Poetry and Settled Status for All

Poetry and Settled Status for All
An Anthology

Edited by Ambrose Musiyiwa

Introduced by Claudia Webbe MP

Civic  Leicester

First published in Great Britain in 2022 by
CivicLeicester
y. https://www.youtube.com/user/CivicLeicester
f. https://www.facebook.com/CivicLeicester
CivicLeicester@gmail.com

ISBN-13: 978-1-9164593-7-3

Dedicated to all who have left the place they were born
to find home elsewhere,
to those who support them, and
to peace and community activist *extraordinaire*
Penny Walker (1950-2021).

.

Contents

ix

Introduction

Poetry and stories help us reach an understanding that we could never have previously imagined. By transporting us into another world, the written word allows us to understand events from another's perspective and provides a unique insight into the world around us and the people within it.

That is the magic of this wonderful anthology of poetry and short prose, organised by CivicLeicester, which focuses on one of the most pressing political issues of our time – the need for permanent residency for all people living in countries like the United Kingdom.

This collection is inspired by how, in Britain and the Irish States, in response to the Covid-19 pandemic, several coalitions, including the Status Now Network, Members of Parliament and groups concerned with the welfare of refugees and migrants, are calling for Settled Status or Indefinite Leave to Remain to be granted to all people who have insecure immigration status or are undocumented or in the legal process, so that the people can access healthcare, housing, food and vaccines. I am proud to be part of this movement, which recognises the humanity and value of everyone – regardless of their country of birth.

I am also incredibly proud to have been born and bred in Leicester, which is a wonderfully diverse city.

Leicester's identity is forged from a history of immigration and welcoming those seeking asylum, with Jewish Russian migrants arriving in the mid-1800s, followed by European Jews fleeing persecution and Nazi barbarism in the 1930s. After the Second World War, Leicester welcomed migrants from the Caribbean and the Indian subcontinent. In the late 1960s and 1970s, thousands of Asian refugees arrived from East Africa, notably those fleeing persecution in Uganda. And, this century, we have hosted refugees and asylum seekers from all over the world.

This is what makes Leicester special. We are the city where the minorities make up the majority. And we are richer for this vibrant exchange of cultures.

But I do not take tolerance and multiculturalism for granted. The right for different communities and cultures to live side by side has been fought for through generations of struggle.

We must continue to do all in our power to fight for a humane immigration and citizenship system in Britain, in the Irish States and around the world. Yet during the coronavirus pandemic, for example, we have seen huge steps backwards by Britain's reactionary government, whose Nationality and Borders Bill is anti-refugee to its core.

Many undocumented people are destitute and living in the shadows, fearful of what will happen to them if they identify themselves. They cannot access healthcare, emergency shelter and food, nor report or seek protection from domestic violence, rape, exploitation, and other awful abuses.

In nearly all cases, undocumented people are not criminals – but simply those who have fallen through the cracks of the government's callous hostile environment policies. In countries of deep, yet vastly unequal wealth, like Britain, we must ensure that everyone - regardless of their immigration status - has their basic needs met.

The collection, *Poetry and Settled Status for All*, includes moving reflections from around the world on the lived experience of being a migrant, an undocumented migrant or seeking refuge. It also powerfully conveys migrant, undocumented migrant and refugee experiences of life, education, housing, work, healthcare, immigration and asylum systems, and the hostile environment.

The beauty of this collection inspires us to redouble our efforts to ensure that everyone has a secure immigration status, without which it is nearly impossible to build a stable and happy life. Because when we stand together, there is nothing we cannot accomplish. As this collection shows, it is up to us to build a society in which everyone is valued – no matter their country of birth.

Claudia Webbe MP
Member of Parliament for Leicester East
Leicester, November 2021

Peter A
Of fish and billionaires

Fish, so it seems, are not required to apply for settled status -
established simply by their choice to swim in British waters.

Am I permitted to enquire why these lowly creatures
are allowed so readily to stay without visas,

Yet humans wishing to improve their lives and our lives
are treated with suspicion and prejudice?

Is my head befuddled, failing so to understand
why we do not wrap our arms around our universal kind?

I am evidently too simple to appreciate
subtleties involved in decisions the powers make,

To exclude or waive barriers as a magician can
for status or money, but not the modest needs of man.

Should we not hold tight those who work hard in return
before the connected and greedy with money to burn,

Who will not pay taxes or support those who need it
but transfer profit offshore where no one can reach it?

We know those in charge will not agree with this analysis
preferring to welcome oligarchs and oblivious fish.

Confronted with policies so inhumane and scandalous, the question is,
Shall we stand for this? Shall we stand for this? Shall we stand for this?

Sandra A Agard
Come Let Me Tell You a Story

Come let me tell you a story
of dreams, hopes and futures cut and tossed in the wind
as the hostile environment ripped through pasts, presents and futures
weaving doubt, hatred, pain, suffering –
fear slithering its way into homes of those who thought
they were safe and free in their Motherland. Free no more
as lives were picked, prodded
and probed. Left to pick up the pieces of shattered lives –
their existence now questioned,
queried,
quizzed,
interrogated.

Come let me tell you a story
where one's life was made difficult
by the denial of dignity and humanity
by successive British Governments.
Where the lack of the right document was seen as just cause
to deny one everything that makes life bearable, passable, liveable.
Words like fairness, justice and trust no longer applied.

Come let me tell you a story
of a people who left sun-kissed islands in search of golden pavements
only to be betrayed by this hostile environment so cruel and unjust.
Children who came on their parents' British passports
stamped with hypocrisy and lies.
Children, now adults, who were asked to look for dusty
ancient school records lost in time.
Children, now with families of their own,
ripped from jobs, homes and lives

only to be locked away in grim detention centres awaiting fate.
Children, now adults, who could not return to bury their Elders
in those sun-kissed islands left so long ago.
Children, who became adults, now sadly passed away
their call for Justice unanswered.

Come let me tell you a story
of a generation betrayed by fake apologies
their songs of freedom stifled and silenced
their truths crushed, scattered, hidden
and ignored.

Come
listen to my story for it is long and must be told.

Are you sitting comfortably?

Once upon a time, many moons ago
ships called Ormonde and Windrush brought hope seekers
onto these shores.
Come
let me tell you their story …

Mayo Agard-Olubo
At The Edge of Our Map

Where are we going, Dad?
Can you show me on our map?

Where we are going, my dear
Is beyond the edge of our map

Will we find safety, beyond the edge of our map?

I do not know, my dear

Will we find a home, beyond the edge of our map?

I do not know, my dear

Will we be welcome, beyond the edge of our map?

I do not know, my dear

So why are we going beyond the edge of the map?

Because I know we cannot stay here
I know it may seem crazy to leave our home behind
I hope where we are going the people will be kind
This map is all we have ever known
And I do not know what we will find
But our home is not safe anymore
This is a journey we must make

It is time to go, my dear
This is risk that we must take
So, take our map, roll it up tight
And keep it in your heart
So even as we leave our home
It will always be part of you
Even in the brand-new place
As we make our new start, a new life
And draw a new map
Together

Advia Ahmed
Beauty Day

It's very early, on a cold Saturday in December.
Filled with caffeine and a little food,
we arrive at the Women and Children's Centre
in The Jungle, in Calais.
Today is Beauty Day.
The image of a salon,
warm, cosy and well lit may come to mind,
with employees in clean uniforms,
perfect hair and perfect nails
ready to serve.
The smell of shampoo, perfume and nail varnish fill the air.
STOP.
In The Jungle,
reality is a dark tent with little light.
A wood burner is lit in the hope it will create some warmth.
In unwashed old joggers, decent-ish hair
and nails with dirt in them,
we are ready.
We welcome 30 women.
I am stationed to do pedicures.
I wash feet and massage them with oil.
I am careful to work around the deep cuts the women have
from climbing fences in the hope of getting to safety.
They feed me and braid my hair
and I wash and massage their feet.
They say I am humble.
For a few hours, we forget where we are.
We talk, laugh and drink coffee.
I do not forget
the torn muddy shoes, the feet, the deep cuts.

They humble me.
In this place that is no place for human beings,
we have a day called Beauty Day.

Jim Aitken
The Citizens of Nowhere

"... if you believe you're a citizen of the world, you're a citizen of nowhere."
Theresa May, Conservative Party Conference, 2016

Stealthily the night crept in
like a black padding cat
all wrapped up in itself.

Ignoring the fading of the light
the blackbird singing said
the force of life must win through.

And I thought of the citizens of nowhere
who continue singing their songs of hope,
keeping the flame inside alive.

The vans that read *Go Home*
could not have applied to them
for they are the citizens of nowhere.

Even though they have lived here for
fifty years or more, their status is
as the people without the papers.

Their ancestors were once transported
across the wild Atlantic waves
to work for nothing as enslaved chattel.

Now their descendants who came
to work in our public services
are the sudden citizens of nowhere.

Like *Joseph K* they stand accused
of being simply who they are –
a mere time-served expendability.

Yet the blackbird has no papers
and needs no permission to sing
for he is native wherever he flies.

Malka Al-Haddad
Refugee and The Home Office

Birdcatcher does not want to give up

Despite all the death that haunts the world

In spite of the coffins scattered looking for a tomb
and the planes parked in airports
deferred tickets
ships that sleep in ports
and frozen roads

despite the knives that tear people's lungs

Despite all the abandoned homes in my homeland
Despite all the fear that glues our walls, doors and windows
Birdcatcher continues to fight butterflies

But we will not give up
because whoever survived the horrors of those wars and siege and saw
corpses scattered on the ground
not deserving of such a trivial end
We are the ones who decide the end

Stay away
Stay away, stop reading hymns of death
Stop stealing the wind from the birds
Life and freedom is for all

Remember your water history
Who took the heads of our heroic warriors
All the palm trees and seedlings left ruin

Remember
if Tony Blair had not stormed my country with his war chariot
I would now be drinking cardamom tea with my brothers
and the children of my neighbourhood

If he had not occupied my country, I would have fallen asleep
on my mother's pillow smelling of incense
and not have suffered the nightmares of the birdcatcher

If George Bush had not occupied my country,
I would not have now shut the doors of my garden
to guard against the infiltration of the birdcatcher

They killed the oil seller in my homeland and left the fires burning till now

whenever I opened my mouth, to talk about my country, rivers, dates
and olives in my country, blood flowed from my lips, the blood is red
and their occupation was a red line

So, remember
I do not want to stay at your cage and weep
I'm thousands of birds in circled flight
We are rebels and claim to not surrender to the reality of injustice
that we do not belong to
Remember
And we will not be silent
We will not be silent

Saffanna Al Jbawi
Under the Jasmine Tree

Do not think I came from the past
or that I do not have an education, history or heart.
Do not look at me as if I am an insect or a rat.
I did not come to stand in a queue
for food and clothes,
maybe old, maybe new.
There I had a lovely house with a garden
and lots of friends.
My students, books, brothers and sisters,
all of them, I lost.
All of them I miss.
Two things I brought:
my children and my coat.
I do not want a flat or flute,
some meat or fruit.
There, under the jasmine tree,
I buried our stories, tears, smiles and memories
for fear they would be stolen like our dreams.
There on the balcony of my house,
I left a cup of coffee and conversation with neighbours.
On the tray, there were some of the jasmine flowers
contaminated by the smell of gunpowder.
My children's clothes are still there on the clothesline
waiting for the sun of hope and the wind of love.
The voices of the neighbour's children
collecting strawberries in my garden
are still singing in my ears.
I ask someone who is still there
to water the flowers
which grow on my mother's grave.
I ask someone to feed our cat
which is waiting for us at the front door.

Saffanna Al Jbawi
The Trip of Death & Shattered Hopes

She folded her tent and chose to leave
For an unknown fate.
She held her son's hand and walked.
All the while she was hiding her tears.

The sun was catching its light,
The autumn leaves scattered.

Her child was cuddling the remains of his doll
He was wondering, where…?
"To the sea...?" he asked.
"Is there another camp?
I love the sea."
In his imagination he started to escape,
Building a sandy castle
And gleaning some shells.

Wretched people thronged there,
To flee or maybe to die?
Too much fear, too little hope.
What after that?
Tired eyes. Broken hearts.
Famished souls.
Dissipated screams.

Got lost in the wind's gusts.
They tasted different types of death.
Their graves were everywhere.
Their boat arrived
But they did not arrive

Haleemah Alaydi
Many Things but a Refugee

Today, you want to be many things but a refugee
A grumpy child, whining
for buying the wrong ice cream flavour.
America for boat riders and drowners,
looking for somewhere to call home.
A new language for those with clumsy English
So that they can pronounce *dream, freedom, home*
better, easier, like a native.

Today, you want to be many things but a refugee
A playful song in a city in ruins,
the blood still fresh from your mother's body.
A faraway God,
hiding a shotgun above the fireplace,
ready to kill, ready to die.

Aryan Ashory
My God

Until when
must I see my Kabul wandering the corners of other countries?
Until when must mothers lose themselves
wandering in forests and on boats?
Where is the milk for this newborn to drink?
Where is the walking stick for the old men?
My God, see how they have strewn my country
to the four corners of the world.
Like this, they propel us outside.
Like this, a mother weeps for her lost darling and children.
The children of my land have never tasted the meaning of childhood.
This country makes them regret they were ever born.
Their eyes have not seen welcome.

Janine Booth
Another Country

The NHS is not another country
Going to clinic's not a trip abroad
Its purpose is for treating not for hunting
No frontiers from reception to the ward
I have to cross the town not cross the oceans
A hospital's no tourist trap now, is it?
Rather than the needles, stitches, lotions
So many other sites I'd rather visit
Not smuggling drugs nor medicines nor pills in
The staff are healers, they're not border guards
I've nothing to declare except my illness
I don't send postcards, I get Get Well cards
- They treat my sickness not my shade of skin
- Why should I need a passport to get in?

Sheena Bradley
Silkworm

A Northern childhood littered with roiling
words like Orange and Green,
Troubles and fear,
border, bigotry and bombs
should have boiled
away my chrysalis skin.

But parents had known family divided
against itself, brother hunting
brother in Civil War.
They wove their fibres,
swathed us in a soft silk of delusion
helped by the geography of religion.
We lived among our own, call it
herd instinct or gerrymandering.

I was eleven when a friend, slighted
because I wouldn't share my skipping rope,
first called me a *Bloody Papish.*
I rushed home to ask what it meant,
what I was and why.

I was eighteen and in Dublin –
a different country
by all accounts,
before discovering
another girl despised me,
not for my religion –
but for my silken complacency.

Lavern Buchanan-Sy
Unsettled, I remain

Unsettled	I remain
Unsettled	it's either loss or gain
Unsettled	my name is not Smith or Jones
Unsettled	my voice has high octave tones
Unsettled	I scream my voice getting louder
Unsettled	my children should be prouder
Unsettled	I have a right to prove
Unsettled	it's either stay or move
Unsettled	I have been here for many years
Unsettled	I remain, still scared my fears worsening
Unsettled	I arrived to serve and to give
Unsettled	all I ask is, give me a chance to live
Unsettled	I am not here seeking welfare benefits
Unsettled	I wait for my permission to settle or my limits
Unsettled	I remain

Helen Buckingham
Haiku

no room at the inn for a pregnant refugee

Lela Burbridge
Daily Faith Hides

Daily faith hides

Drafty box room,
Waits for news,
No one asks her story.

Too tired to fight,
Months ricocheting,
Between dank offices.

One application,
Handed to Uniforms,
Fate decided by strangers.

The Privileged disbelieve
What her eyes witnessed,
Disbelieve her life in danger.

The heavy memory,
Husband, children
Slaughtered, disease.

If denied leave to remain,
Shall she end?
Die by her own hand

No longer persecuted,
Proud her man
Stood against corruption?

Haunted by nightmares,
Feet telling her to run,
She dreams to live.

Her mind set:
Reconstruct a life
From broken pieces.

Stay in sanctuary.
Be a Citizen.
Start over.

Richard Byrt
A Nineteen-Hour Day for a Tin of Spam and a Bottle of Coke

Who would have missed me if I had jumped?
But you told me you would take care of me
if I went with you to Green Acres.
It sounded peaceful, so I climbed down
from the bridge. When we reached Leighton Buzzard, you said,
"Forget your family, I am your Pa."
You shaved my head, forced me to wear
a uniform just like the others.
Forced me to asphalt, build roads, clean your chalet:
a nineteen-hour day for a tin of Spam and a bottle of Coke.
Beat me when I demanded my pay.
Told me if I ran off, you would catch me. Catch me and kill me.

And then the raid before dawn: the sudden
swoop. Cops stormed in.
Found me asleep in the horsebox.

Set me free. But where do I go?
Where do I go to now?

"...The only people willing to employ [people seeking asylum] are those happy to do so illegally..." Stephen Harris (2019). How UK asylum system creates perfect conditions for modern slavery and exploitation to thrive. *The Conversation*, 8 April 2019

"...a man had been sitting on... a bridge, ready to commit suicide, when he was spotted by the gang, and brought to the site..." Maev Kennedy (2011). Leighton Buzzard "slave" empire uncovered in major police raid. *The Guardian*, 11 September, 2011

In the UK, many victims and survivors of modern slavery and trafficking also face deportation to their countries of origin, with limited access to adequate legal representation, and Home Office decisions based on inadequate evidence. This occurs, even though they are likely to be re-enslaved or face other serious risks following deportation.

M Chambers
Unsettled

At the meeting for refugees,
People were greeted by name.
It seemed that everyone knew everyone.
Organisations in bed with one another.
Is this how you feel?
Like a voyeur?
Looking in on unfamiliar worlds,
yet not a part of them.
Years it seems since I took the bus.
For you, perhaps, a wonder.
A bus departing and arriving safely,
Without attack; without incident.
A revelation
that I, since a child, had forgotten.
Drowning in the tediousness of safety,
We fear your reminder
That life is not supposed to be easy.
Harder to rehearse our imaginary pains,
When one, lately escaped from Hell,
is selling Big Issues on the corner by the crossing.
The soft ululating ripples of heterogeneous accents
wash over me in a kindly wave.
Dashed by the dagger of difference,
As one destroys your safety with,
"You're not from around here, are you?"
I wish you gone.
I wish you safe in some comfortable haven.
A happy refuge where your image is forgotten.
Returning me to the banality of everyday routine.

Your smiling headscarf
unsettling, disturbing.
Your absence a sense of loss.
A hole left on the familiar High Street;
I shall miss your cheerful, "Good morning!"

A C Clarke
In Transit

The wind flowers in the water ... in my hands. Rainie Oet

The wind is whipping water-lilies out of the waves –
so she imagines,
sensing the ship's roll ten minutes from harbour, her eyes tight shut
on a vision of ricefields, ponds alive with blossom,
the home which is her soul,
even here.

She's standing at the altar, the heart of the house; her mother
lights candles before a photograph –
the *ba ngoai* whose engulfing softness
kept her out of the clutches of nightmare, routed the demons
lurking in the rafters.
Incense sweetens the air. She can almost smell it
even here.

A sideways lurch throws her against her neighbour. Throws
her neighbour on the other side against her.
A pang of nausea. Heat is climbing.
People begin to beat the walls, to use their precious breath
to call out. Her mother bows three times.
She thinks she hears a voice, ghost-thin, speaking her name,
a voice of comfort
even here.

How kind the sun is in the evening, when it blesses
the courtyard. She sits here often
after the day's toil. Peace. She is dreaming peace.
Wedged between hot bodies, her lungs fighting for air,

her fingers now too weak
to key a farewell message, she feels a light breeze stir
the betel trees. A leaf-frond strokes her cheek.
Her village reaches out its hands.
Even here.

A C Clarke
What a performance

She's performing need, performing abjection, hands clasped, head bowed, in one unbroken curve of supplication, her rickety collecting tin an echo of the beakers on the table behind her (which is not a real table), from one of which spirals a straw (which is not a real straw), at the end of which is the zippered mouth of a shark, (not a real shark), performing the action of sucking up non-existent water.

They're all on benefits you know. We should give to our own.

She's performing need, the way someone abroad without the language performs "where can I find somewhere to eat?" She's a piece of street furniture people manoeuvre around, with a glance at the shark and the beakers that registers nothing. The street is full of intentions, not all of them good.

She has a gold tooth in her mouth. Must be worth something! We should give to our own.

She's performing need. Performs day in, day out, hard graft for slow returns. Someone knocked out the shark and beakers over a cup of coffee, just one more job for the advertising agency, who don't come cheap.

Liz Clegg
Letter to Jamil

Jamil,
I've packed another bag for you tonight.
I've managed to find a really good sleeping bag this time. It's cold.
I remembered the bin bags. Please use them. It will help you keep a bit
        drier.
There's two pairs of socks and a torch in the side pocket.
I've put in some snacks and 5 euros.
Please don't lose your phone again.

Jamil,
I'm scared.
I'm scared I'm going to lose you.
The forms they've given me don't have a box for you,
and no one's prepared to change this.

You have to be clever in this game, Jamil.
You have to talk the talk, understand complex law;
They don't want to hear about our lives, our daily routine
of keeping you dry and fed and out of trouble.
They're not interested in the nightly ritual of watching you leave "to try"
        get to the UK,
let alone acknowledge the panic I feel
because I may never know what became of you,
or worse still, you join the growing list
of those who died trying.

Jamil,
I beg you,
please listen to me.
Don't get into the refrigerated lorries. Wait for something safer.
Massoud was older. He still died.

I can't promise to solve this,
but I'm trying.

Jamil,
I love you dearly,
never finished,
and I will fight to the bitter end to keep you safe.

Mark Connors
All Aboard

Yes, this is the correct platform.
Yes, the train is going where you think it is.
Yes, it will be overcrowded.
Don't worry about keeping the aisles free.
Please refrain from smoking.
Please don't squeeze children through the sliding windows.

Please take all your belongings with you.
Please take all your children with you.
Yes, this is the final stop.
Yes, you are still within our borders.
Yes, I'm afraid we were lying.
No, the soldiers are here for *your* safety.

No, we are not sorry for lying.
No, you are here so we can process you.
No, this is not the forties all over again.
Yes, we do have food and water.
But please refrain from chanting.
Please refrain from emotional blackmail.

No, we don't want you to stay.
Yes, you can walk 100 miles along the motorway.
Please keep the hard shoulder clear.
Yes, we have kind people in our country.
Yes, some will give you food and water.
Thank you for passing through. Have a safe onward journey.

Robin Daglish
Asylum Seeker

I have known a continent of loss,
deserts and seas I've crossed,
walked the endless road.

I'm wandering the pavements,
wondering what city to wear today,
what weather to wear on my face.

I'm a skeleton of fear,
why did I come here,
my life is a court case.

Justice has a deaf ear,
a luxury word:
the luxury of lawyers.

The final impediment:
the reams of forms and documents,
glacial decisions of governments.

A silty river of jungle flotsam flows,
quiet in my veins.
My mind is a swamp
of summer rains.

Now I face my final dread:
Leave to Remain,
or being sent back
again.

Catherine Davidson
Flag

I had lived in this country a long time
before I noticed you: on April 23, 2015
two boy professors proudly raised you

over lunch. It was your English day. You'd
been hiding in the British splash, a cross
with no blue: blank white, red like blood.

I wondered how you felt about yourself?
Down in Kent in 2017, you flew overhead;
on the roofs of many houses, you made us

nervous as we walked the nature reserve,
the shipwreck hut graffiti slogan shouted:
No "Rape – U – Gees!" loud on the shingle.

Were you proud of yourself then? Red
as a face blocked with anger. White knight
slaying a dragon, rescuing a princess, who

wouldn't be proud of that? Later, another
travelling scholar rooted you in the Levant,
Turkish Christian version of an older myth:

Apollo slaying Delphi's snakes, killing oracles,
original patriarch conquering chthonic fears;
I felt proud of our mutual Mediterraneanism.

Had I got you all wrong? At a Ligurian port
I saw you draped on every window. Scanning
for choler, I found a trader, the flag of Genoa,

Malta's open harbours, history without violence
like England's perpetually losing teams, a land
with no winners, proud to be a part, flapping.

Emer Davis
Mule

When the door closes behind me
I reach out to the air and grab
onto tiny specks of freedom,
minute grains of dust
streaming through my hands.
Imprisoned by a wall of silence,
I breathe this air and listen
to the faint hum of barbed voices
fighting to be heard all around me.

Day after day I will enter this space,
year after year I will live out
my sentence in this small cubicle
looking at an old faded snapshot
of smiling faces at home,
shut away from you all.

This is where I can think freely,
This is where I can find peace,
This is where I can begin to live again.

Gone are the harsh words and tones,
Gone are the lightning slaps and bruised flesh,
Gone are the enquiring looks and tormented eyes.

No more hovering footsteps or blood stained sheets,
No more cries and shouts,
No more hands pleading with him to stop.

I left all that behind the day I walked away,
limping with my suitcase of shattered dreams,
I boarded the flight of no return
believing I could be free.

Emer Davis
Resurrected

Trapped in the crossfire,
we travelled across many terrains,
our past sewn into the lining of our coats,
the future wrapped in plastic around our necks,
we drifted on the horizon,
unable to see the shadows,
searching for our remains,
unable to hear the last breath
from our neighbours,
unable to smell the decomposed flesh
floating below,
our straw filled life jackets
rippled across the sea,
a strong arm grasping onto us,
we shuffled towards the porta cabin,
drenched in the tears of those we left behind,
we shuffled slowly to a new life,
our garments discarded across the Aegean Sea.

And, now, I look at my children,
jumping across clumps of barren bog,
purple heather sprinkled through their hair,
the sun declining in this new land,
planting a seed in a small field in Mayo,
we watch it grow,
and, remember the scorched earth
we left behind,
nurturing this new blossom,
we breathe new life into this soil,
moistened with the tears from our past.

John Davison
The Diplomats' Façade

Don't put your trust in smugglers
Who cast-off in the night,
They may not know or give a damn
If their boats are watertight.

Don't try forcing the doors of a truck
While the driver takes his break,
When the air gets thin you'll be out of luck
Though it seemed like a piece-of-cake.

The cold stores of our stately homes
Are stocked with grouse and pheasant,
We celebrate our heritage
To distract us from the present.

We've severed ties with Brussels,
And stormed off in a huff,
We've tried extending open arms,
But now we've had enough.

You might think we're a bastion of decency,
Where culture and justice are treasured,
But we've downgraded our hospitality,
By your earning potential you're measured.

We're writing a set of criteria,
Like Canada did and Australia.
If you don't have the skills that we're seeking
Then we shall look upon you as a failure.

If you swim across the Dover Straits
Big ships you'll be avoidin'
But you'll need official paperwork
For those interviews in Croydon.

Don't go hiding under a train
With a harness on a hook,
When it speeds through the night you'll be in for a fright,
You may wish you were back in Tobruk.

I'll say it again, though we left it too late,
We are writing a list of criteria
And then we'll determine if you are our mate,
Or if you're to be labelled inferior.

Don't try crawling up our stony beaches
To the sunlit promenade,
We now treat migrants much like leeches
Behind the diplomats' façade.

Theoni Dourida
In the hole

From a toxic oleander hangs our merriment,
withered at 37 ° C.
How we ended up here?
The haul was long.
In the beginning
they turned our homes into matchboxes.
Gunpowder and blackened thoughts
our amalgam of the grind.
Hereupon,
loaded with signatures,
algorithms and passports
the walls one day just cloaked the skies.
Our nostrils bled and our fists clenched.
We ourselves,
the privileged ones,
nudged the little finger of the drowned
and blushed before the locked gates.
Now all the roads are going uphill.
We're in the hole,
but money is the least.
Ruthless usurers ourselves,
panting for the last resort
on the borderline.

Alan Dunnett
Succour

We have nowhere to live.
                    I sympathise -
I can't get on the housing list.
                    No food -
we have nothing to eat.
                    I'm hungry too -
and my kids have it rough.
                    We would have died -
we had to get out.
                    I sympathise, mate -
but we've got problems here.
                    My brother died -
I have his children with me...
                    I've got kids -
I blame the eurozone...
                    and his young wife -
old before her time.
                    Heating bills are pants -
this isn't paradise.
                    I feel your pain -
God be with you.
                    Try good old Germany -
they owe us one.
                    Thank you. Thanks. May we just
step inside and use your toilet?
                    The flush -
it's busted. Try number ten. Top, top bell.

Attracta Fahy
Beautiful One
For Ifeoma

I followed the line, red like an artery.
"Nightmares are the worst," she said,
"always a bat biting my neck, the lions' roar,
and the guns."

Eight years old, I saw my whole family
shot. An old man took me in: "Fourteen years
I had two babies."

Nothing to give but my ear, boned bridge
between her world and mine. The sun shadowed
her face, dusk velvet skin, well of her eyes
sunk into ravines, as she spoke of her children:
"They think I'm dead."

"I was taken under the premise of work,
ten years before I escaped, got myself here."
She was the eye of the desert she'd crossed
to another bleak country, sharing a room
with four other women, cleaned houses for money.

"I'm just a number," she said, "The Red Cross
cannot search, find them, until I have asylum."
Four years.

Her voice like a violin in a distant room;
I stormed terrors by day, ran from them at night.
There's a cathedral in everyone, our own religion.
The reason we become evil is no one will listen,
hold: a chalice, for the suffering of our wounds.

Dark continually folding over light, I climbed
walls, reached to ceilings, held candles, my heart
a stained glass window, host to love, and betrayal.
My altar the feet that brought me over sands,
fierce waves, the moon rising, pulling me on.

I am always running, even as I sit here,
close my eyes, see a young girl, braids in her hair,
crying for her dead mother, children not yet born.
A child chasing red sandy tracks, orange dust
at her heels.

I still smell the hunger, the lion's famishment,
sun setting to the music of night time drums,
the sound of gunfire still rings through my body.

Hope kept me going, taking from each day
what dawn had to offer.

Max Terry Fishel
My mother, smoking

Her:

Those queasily green-packeted
menthol cigarettes (one giving me

my sly first sinful taste up the
chimney), smoked with coal-

black coffee, she never gasped.
Reading, elbow-propped, clouded

by steam and smoke, the grim line
of her mouth made her face shrink

as mounds of tangled Jews piled
before her on the front room carpet.

Me:

No siblings, I turned to my friends
for normalcy, hoping they would

not exterminate me. Facially, I
was probably safe, but that

surname, always a risk. Coming
home from school I tasted her

smoke; it was not the smoke of
Auschwitz, but still my alveoli

twitched, trembled at this invasion
as surely as the march of war.

.

My mother was forced to leave Düsseldorf in 1939, and fled to Switzerland for the duration of World War 2, after which she came to England.

44

Paul Francis
Balancing the Books

The old traditions are a luxury.
To win back UKIP votes, sod sanctuary,
ditch "each case on its merits" pieties.
Incentives to the staff for getting rid –
chocolates, cake, your photo on the wall.

Make up the shortfall anyway you can.
Leave to remain? Two hundred and fifty quid
to process – but it costs them ten times that.
In Germany, a five-year visa costs
a twentieth of what we charge.

A deportation flight is twenty grand
so we outsource it: "Hey – deport yourselves!"
We'll buy their ticket, throw in extra cash.
Can't work, can't rent, can't use the NHS;
make it so hard to stay they'd rather go.

Sometimes the cut and paste can get unstuck –
like the Jamaican guy we said had failed
"to prove he was at risk back in Iraq."
Though maybe that would be a safer choice
since five Jamaicans we sent back got killed.

Nobody's safe. Six died in channel boats
(plus thirty that we kept in custody).
The Public Health said barracks were a risk -
Covid, asylum seekers, dormitories...
a hundred and ninety cases, up to now.

A better class of migrant's what we want.
Who needs careworkers when you could have skills?
Twenty-five grand a year's the minimum.
Three grand per visa, which could take six months;
an extra thousand and we'll speed it up.

The money's rolling in – and sloshing out.
There's compensation for the detainees
that we got wrong – that's twenty million quid.
But then we go again, appeal. Again
they say we got it wrong, more money out.

The sums aren't simple, but the lesson's clear.
Don't see a doctor, go to school
or call the police – that's how we'll track you down.
Whatever is in doubt one certainty
remains: the scent of terror in the air.

Birgit Friedrich
Divorce

Your Motherland holds my children,
sends me home and
leaves me to
drown
in the sea between us.

Birgit Friedrich
Sterntaler

I do not know your truth, the memories are yours
to lose. You do not want me to imagine the moment when soldiers
arrived on your street. You are five when you smell the burning skies,
hear the snow crush under their feet, leaving footprints of the silenced
behind them. You find yourself in darkness under a cold sky with stars
        unmoved
by corpses drowned under the ice, cracked by the weight of their homes
        tied on sledges.
You carry the image frozen in your mind heavy as the steps you take
with
        your tired feet.
The boots are too big for you. Your mother had filled in the gaps
with soft socks to smooth your way through the drifting snow, and when
        you cry
she holds on to your hand, keeps you awake telling you tales mothers of
        mothers
had told their children, and you to me, about a girl lost in the woods
deep in the night giving her last piece of clothing to those with the least.
And when the girl looks up to the moon the stars drop down
as golden coins. When you look up, steel bullets fall instead.

Stephanie F Goodacre
Snakes and Ladders

My country has plenty venomous snakes, vipers hide everywhere
ready to strike at the heart of our lives, disguised as familiar faces
organised for attack. Run, never look back.

Unexpected turns, dead ends, steep climbs, a chance escape
passage paid, asylum sought, hurdles faced, questions posed
no rights without answers, right answers.

Long slow climb, no idea how many rungs, ladder scaled, claim
leave to remain, to remain where I am, not there yet, not quite safe
set back again, again, again.

Dearest kin, so young, we hugged until you slept, I crept out
promised I would be back. All those years, so many tears
since I fled - you still alive my precious ones?

Help at hand, face legal snakes, twists and turns, ups and downs
kindness of an outstretched hand, a sanctuary friend
guides me through forms, so many forms.

I've climbed rungs, jumped hoops, lived through doubts
hung on to threads that my three are not dead, five years here
fears give way, here to stay.

Good news, Red Cross traced my brood, my precious blood
plan to reunite, putting everything in place, entry rights,
chaperoned flights, reunion in sight.

Celebration, jubilation oh deflation. New variant strikes
homeland on red list, border clampdown, need pre-flight tests
hotel quarantine, they insist, insist.

Back to square one, legal windows shift, who knows if each step
reunites, or another rung will break, I hang on, life on hold
another day I wait, still fearing snakes.

Anne Goodwin
Miles of Mountain, Miles of Sand

"Go home!" they hissed, when she left the high-rise, dragging a child by each hand. Did her headscarf offend them, or the coffee tint of her skin? Yet their condolences confused her further: they said she'd survived through grit? Checking the dictionary in the refugee centre, the words didn't match the nightmare in her head.

Miles of mountain, miles of sand, miles of water in a leaky boat. Robbed of her dollars, repeatedly raped, grit was the stone in her shoe, the rock on the road to safety.

Barrington Gordon
running in the dark

we're running in the dark
we're running in the light
we're running   don't look back
behind is pain and strife

we're running not to get caught
we're running because we bought
a ticket to the promised land
we're running   holding daddy's hand

we're running   no time to stop
to pick up that precious doll I dropped
in the dirt now trodden down
by soldiers' boots from beyond our village and town
trees burn loud   horns grimly blare

we're running   can't catch my breath
Mum says stay ahead of death
I am tired   hungry and cold
Dad says don't worry be bold

we're running and I want to be brave
we're running so as not to be slaves
we're running to be free
we're running   I just want to see

the boats up on the horizon
so small   a ticket to die for
we're running and I don't want to give up
but I'm exhausted and just want to stop

GPT-2
Indefinite Leave to Remain for All

Indefinite Leave to Remain for All
In the state of nature, at night
Its color, sweet and fair
The brightness of the morning,
The glory of the sun, the calm of
The birds, the magic of the wind,
The endless.

Submitted by researchers from Center for Humans and Machines at the Max Planck Institute
for Human Development, Nils Köbis and Luca Mossink, this poem was generated by GPT-2 (a
deep learning model from OpenAI) that was fine-tuned on a 1.2MB text file containing
poems from Maya Angelou, Robert Frost, Jane Campion, Roald Dahl and William Blake. For
more information on the work Köbis and Mossink are doing,
see: https://doi.org/10.1016/j.chb.2020.106553

Joachim Grevel
The Hoard

I hoard the scraps of paper in a box.
I have no rights as stranger in this land.
The pending hymn and pledge – I fear the mock.

Not law nor rule of land came as a shock.
But in a crowd, we feel like ewe and lamb.
I hoard the scraps of paper in a box.

The monarchy, she runs like wheel and cog.
Acceptance, cheerful subjects, no demands.
The pending hymn and pledge – I fear the mock.

Democracy and freedom are a hoax.
Just drink another pint, but no I can't.
I hoard these scraps of paper in a box.

No worries, one more year, I check the clock.
Can't hug my former friends, please understand.
The pending hymn and pledge, I fear the mock.

I struggle, but the exit I can't find.
And blindness holds me, I am damned.
I hoard these scraps of paper in a box.
The pending hymn and pledge, I fear the mock.

Laura Grevel
Girl Walking Across Europe

Let's watch a girl walk across Europe:
walk across Europe with a backpack and a cat named Hermaniwab,
and as she walks people join her,

not to tell her to go home, not to warn her off the borders,
but to give her flowers and biscotti and an embroidered cloak,
and to walk beside her across the boot of Italy,
where the sea captain did not get arrested for saving her from the
        sinking boat
but was lauded and crowned with roses,

where the embroidered girl walks on with Hermaniwab,
to arrive at the Austrian border
where she is not sent to a refugee camp,
but where the Chancellor greets and gifts her with a handsome horse-
        drawn carriage,
where she rides and parades with a brass band
through a Vienna that throws her kisses,

where at the city's edge she gets out and asks to walk on,
calling Hermaniwab to her side,
walking along the Danube,
with blue in her hair and honey on her lips.

Where she waltzes on,
copper skin shining, singing an ancient chant.

Laura Grevel
Advice From a Foreign Stranger Who Settled

Remember to keep your receipts!
The directions are complicated.
Did you arrive in time? Too early, too late?
Did you arrive with receipts?
Bring all receipts!

Send in originals, do not tweet:
passports, lab reports, birth certificates, marriage certificates,
receipts of living here for the past five years.
Copies will not be accepted!
Receipts: for the butcher, the baker, the candlestick maker,
for shirts and skirts, shoes and loos, petrol and bread rolls,
electricity and any necessity.
For everything you do, provide evidence!
Which gives the precedence to earn residence,
thus to avoid familial exodus.

Remember to keep your receipts!
The directions are complicated.
Your application must be complete.
Any errors will result in rejection.
But do not let your heartbeat suffer down the
backstreet of paperwork's balance sheet.

The labyrinth is a conceit
that you must try to defeat.
Your goal is to remain,
be the athlete who conquers this domain,
who does not find himself obsolete,
put squarely in the ejection seat.
Remember to keep your receipts!

Laura Grevel
A Foreign House

To be settled
is not something
a piece of paper will ever give.

To be settled
means to hear the voice of a grandmother
the meow of your cat
the wind that greeted your birth.

To be settled
means the heavy beat of rain on roof
the smell of beans and corn bread
the creak of a wooden floor
the beat of a well-known song
the days carried in your pockets.

To be settled
is not to forget the loneliness
of this new place.

To be settled
does not mean the dregs of old life
slowly sink to the bottom of your soul—
never permanently—
for one breath, one memory, one word,
causes the flurry and storm
that tosses mountains.

Rosario Guimba-Stewart
Where We Find Ourselves

They shout, Run and don't look back
No matter what, just carry on
Never stop, never ask
There are no answers
We must look for a safe place

We arrived but still we're lost
We remember the dark nights and the cold wind
The stony faces and unfriendly places

It is not our fault
You must believe us
We didn't choose to leave
We never wanted to be homeless, stateless, fatherless and motherless
We didn't ask for the tanks, the bombs and the guns
We never wanted hunger, torture and death

We breathe but we have no life
We live for the moment
What future we have
We cannot tell, we cannot guess

Monique Guz
Visas 1-5

Silly me
Applying to a UK university
What's another student loan?

"You can apply for a Tier 1 visa upon graduating," they said
"You can remain in the UK for up to 2 years," they said
What was I thinking?

To be honest,
More time with you

Silly us
What were we thinking?

Falling in love
In the middle of a recession

"They ended the Post Study Work scheme," they said
"You'll have to complete your studies from the US," they said
No refunds

I couldn't afford a return flight ticket
Because the landlord wouldn't return my deposit

I couldn't focus on my UK studies
Because I couldn't find a US job

I couldn't sleep at night
Because I couldn't return to homelessness

I couldn't end this
More time with you

Silly you
What were you thinking?

Silly me
Accepting your proposal

Silly us
Unemployed graduates
In a long-distance engagement

Who makes £18,600 fresh out of school?
Who saves £62,500 in a gig economy?

Your pixelated face and delayed voice sustains me
Between student loans, redundancies, and a shared room
In the basement of my friend's passive-aggressive parents' house

Two years later, one of us makes it past the six-month mark with the
        same employer
And one of us has to leave everything and everyone behind
Silly me

Monique Guz
Visas 5-6

My fiancee visa was approved

But my grandmother died
And my mother lost her job
And my sister doesn't understand why everyone is so upset

This is not the time to move
But it took two years to get here

If I don't move now,
The rules will change
And the costs will rise

It's too much to risk

I move into your room
Your sister is across the hall
Your parents are downstairs

This is not where we met
Nor where we lived
Nor where our friends and memories are

This place is different
I am different

Everyone is staring at me
But no one wants to talk

We get married
But have no choice in the wheres, whens or hows

It takes place in an office with my in-laws
And it's over in less than twenty minutes

It feels so sterile and sad
But at least ours wasn't raided by the Home Office

We have a "mini-moon" 25 miles away
And plan a second wedding
We will have it our way this time next year

But the fiancee visa expired
Upon our *I dos*
And we will have to apply
For a spouse visa
And US student loans don't care about my UK work restrictions

Our first year of marriage is me feeling like a burden to you, my
        "sponsor"
And your family, who house me, under a stiff upper lip

I miss *my* family
They force smiles behind a screen
I hide tears behind a phone

I am here, there, both, neither

Monique Guz
Visas 6-7

"I don't want her to serve me, she's a foreigner!" he says
My manager responds to this by letting someone else serve him
I break down in tears – only to hear him mutter something under his
breath
"That's what I get for hiring so many women"

My applications are more successful with your surname
But my interviews are futile – they've decided before I've spoken – and
I'm left with anything I can get (usually abuse)
Who am I to complain?
You are always getting abused at your job – yet you stay because we
won't be eligible for the next few visas without it
Your family doesn't believe my stories and your friends ignore me (they
aren't racist but … I'm a good immigrant)
I don't want to be around them anymore
Let's start our own family – or not – who starts a family when the scope
of your future is just 2.5 years?

We have our second wedding – the one we get to have our way
But one half is staring at the other half – the side that needed financial
assistance to be here today

We move into our own flat and rarely leave it
We have to sit tight between rent, student loans, transaction fees, and
subsequent visas
Besides, the world is getting darker around us

One day, there is a referendum (but I cannot vote) and the Polish shop down the road is set ablaze
I tell my husband I can't live here anymore, but messages of love and solidarity soon fill the windows and I stay

At the end of 2.5 years, we apply for another 2.5 years and rinse our savings – the applications cost more and more
We can only live for the right nows in the shadows of the what-ifs
Another 2.5 years later, we apply for Indefinite Leave to Remain –
the applications cost more and more

I study UK history and pass a Life in the UK test but the "right" answers feel wrong
I apply for Indefinite Leave to Remain as new friends move away to more inclusive cities and countries
I attend biometrics appointments 50 miles away before a "no appeals" announcement is made by the Home Office

There is an election (but I cannot vote)
And the people, the friends who witnessed us suffer, vote to sustain our suffering

We choose love in a hostile environment – even as our spirits are breaking, just as intended

One day, my name is deliberately mispronounced at my own citizenship ceremony
They think I am crying because I am happy for the certificate – but I am grieving the time I will never get back
Everything we suffered – everyone who didn't make it as far as we did – with the privileges we had – why?

I apply for a British passport straight after the ceremony - as soon as it comes, I will book a flight
To the US – to see my mother and my sister – to the Philippines – to see my father
They never could afford flights to the UK

But we enter lockdown the following week – and go on furlough – before finally being made redundant
And I watch my parents age through a screen – through a pandemic, a recession, political unrest, and racism

And wait
And wait
And wait

Can I sponsor them and care for them here? Or will I have to risk losing my citizenship to care for them, abroad?
Should we start a family? In the middle of a recession? 7 years before the climate catastrophe? Where?

Kim Hackleman
I Too Am an Immigrant

The gasps from their mouths shocked me.
"Oh, no, she didn't!" they cried.
I was not prepared for them to feel that this label...
this label that I hold dear,
I was unprepared for it to be taken as an insult.

It ties me to hot sticky summers,
the watermelon that she loved,
to corn you can eat without cooking,
and dancing in hot rain.

The gas man mentioned as he stood in my home:
"I do not like those who are not from here."
I whispered that I, too, was not.
"That doesn't count," he said.
This second blow, invisible.

I was taken back to the fall
(I know you do not call it that)
and the cornucopia she would arrange,
shapes and colours spilling out,
giving thanks, a circle of hands clasping hands.

"I hope you and your baby crash and die!"
they said as they swore out my nationality.
Shaking, holding in the tears, I strapped him in
and tried to make my way home, but failed,
for the only home I longed for in that moment was 3,960 miles away.

The winter cold is dry,
snowball fights, seeing breath,
breaking off an icicle to keep until the spring.
The stories of her on a sled
being pulled behind her father's car on a frozen lake,
these will not be replicated here.

"You fucking cunt."
said calmly, perhaps in jest, but confusing,
as how could it be my fault that he is president
if I did not cast a vote for him?

The spring there…
the dogwood trees at breakfast,
lilies-of-the-valley she pressed and sent,
white blossom carpet in Collett Park looking like warm winter.
The march of snowdrops, crocuses, daffodils
on both sides of the pond bring with them annually eternal hope.

Zsófia Hacsek
Rite of Passage

Grab your phone and download the app
Hold it to the photo page of your passport
Enter the number and wait for the code
Open the text message. Enter six numbers
Put the phone on top of the passport
Hold the phone high and scan your face in
Take a selfie. Hey, where are your eyes?
Freezing? Restarting? Start over
With a little luck, it will work the tenth time
Then perhaps you will secure your place in this strange land

"Rite of Passage" was translated from "Átmeneti rítus", the Hungarian original, by the author.

Nusrat M Haider
Windrush Fate

After 40 years of service
I get the sack
for being
a Windrush passenger
and Black

I am the son
of the ruined coloured empire

Mother country to us
in the detention centre
today at us shouts
and of us tires

Detention centre will deport us
to Kingston port

Churchill once said
we were uncivilised tribes
but then needed us
in both wars
and on the frontline

The hostile environment
left us like dusty books on a shelf

Policy changes likes a river
when it suits

Dimming us down
taking us for fools and clowns
constantly
mockery and intimidation

Is this a nation with no shame?

Steve Harrison
In the Wake of Frobisher

As tides turn
we'll try to fathom
how he made those ocean odysseys
with such primitive equipment and mad bravery.
What waves pushed him out
Which tide pulled him in?
And

       Will rhymers add another verse to
       "Columbus sailed the ocean blue
       In fourteen hundred and ninety-two"?

With

       "People and pilgrims
       guided by fear, faith or stars
       buoyed up with dodgy life jackets
       bought in seedy seaside bars.

       Will Johnny Depp portray you
       as adventurous buccaneers?
       Will School houses be named
       in honour of these modern pioneers?

       Will your names be writ large
       on globes and maps, schools and seas
       will we celebrate the travels
       of last year's refugees?"

Martin Frobisher was a Yorkshire born 16th Century, sailor, navigator, "privateer" and later
the name of a tutor group at the secondary school I attended.

Etzali Hernández
what I remember most of great britain

I remember spending one night in a police cell after my asylum claim
was refused.

I remember being driven 6 hours away from my partner and friends into
a place in the middle of nowhere.

I remember being locked up in a huge wing in an old hunting estate with
other women.

I remember guards making fun of those who didn't speak English or
were wearing a hijab or were visibly queer.

I remember being submerged in the darkness and finding it easier to
imagine jumping out of the window than pulling myself back to light.

I remember seeing people lose themselves in the black hole of a system
that does not see us.

Alice Herve
The Courtesy of Strangers

Our stories are as frayed and ragged as the meagre threads
of blankets in the first camp that offered us refuge.
Our children scrapped after food with wild dogs and untethered
goats. They were cold and hungry even in their dreams.
While all around us spooled out the stories of strangers
just like us, only the smallest of facts shifting, details slipping.

Perhaps the bombs came from the north not the south, slipping
through the skies like a personal vendetta. Threads
of smoke streaming, eyes streaming, the children of strangers
screaming, just as our children screamed. This refuge
has mustered us like cattle, with our former dreams
untenable and the chain of our ancestral line untethered.

Universal human flotsam, we've come untethered
from the networks of goodwill; seeing compassion slipping
like a mask from hostile citizens who hound our dreams.
All we possess now are uncertainties, unattached threads
of what was once interwoven, as we plead for refuge
amongst the cold excuses of unsympathetic strangers.

They are confident that ruin only rains on strangers'
heads, outsiders, from unknown cities, untethered
from real civilization, real culture. But this refuge
houses strange bedfellows. The once high slipping
low and the low finding familiarity in the threads
of clothing, the new kinds of hunger, and the old lost dreams.

Torture is levelling. Even if we nurtured dreams
of escape, we knew we'd be changed. Strangers
invaded our bodies. Pummelled firm flesh into threads.
Tore the spirit from the substance and left it untethered
in a no-man's-land of pain. Our sanity was slipping
out of reach and all we knew was to seek refuge.

When we escaped, we walked and walked until refuge
came to mean only respite from motion. Our former dreams
of comfort, or safety, or welcome, slowly slipping
away until all we asked for was the courtesy of strangers,
the end of abuse, the right to untortured, untethered
freedom; and this bread, this water, these threads.

Someday, we will find refuge with gentler strangers
in a future where harsh dreams drift away, untethered,
and vanish like thistledown slipping from its threads.

Alice Herve
We are all migrants

We are all migrants,
or our ancestors were.
The globe is a web of scarification
where footfall fell crossing continents.
As a hand that has flexed betrays anguish
so the contours of the earth speak of passage.
Bones lie under ice and under ocean
and new roads do little to camouflage
old graves.
Belonging is not our inheritance.
Our forebears were fugitives from ruination,
from flood and famine
from frost and ferocity
from fear and the fervour of those whose gods bedevilled them.
They sought their fortune
or they sought deliverance.
They survived long journeys,
or we would not be here.
I'm not asking you to walk a mile in the shoes of a migrant
only to look back over the many miles our people came
in search of sanctuary
and to leave the door open.

Alice Herve
The Child on The Beach

There are children's treasures on the beaches
tendered on the salt spumed eddies of the dawn
nestled in the ripples of the morning sand
the gifts of the waves are multiform.
Limbs of driftwood beaten into sculpture
from the decking of a perished yacht
and pebbles that vie with gemstones
transformed into crystalline rock,
but the salt rough lick of a kitten can turn
to a ferocious leonine pounce
when the wind picks up and the weather wilds
and the sea pounds breakers on the coast.
Shoes that have lost their partners
and indestructible man-made flotsam
vie with shreds of ravaged dinghies
and the debris shipwrecks jettison.
And the shoes that have lost their partners
belong to those who have lost their all
and the child on the beach is a dead child
who will hunt for treasure no more.

Angi Holden
Extrapolation

I was in the chandler's the first time it happened.
I'd gone in to buy a cleat, so while the staff were busy
I cruised round the aisles. The lad with the ginger hair,
the one who knows the tide tables and the weather forecast,
was helping a father and daughter choose a life-preserver.
The ones they'd already tried lay scattered round their feet,
discarded, like those abandoned across Greek beaches.
And as the child bounced between the shelves,
the orange jacket tied snugly around her small body,
I saw her bobbing away from the boat, her mother
calling her name, weeping into the salt water.
Now it happens all the time: in the street,
in the supermarket, in the school playground.
I see children, even the lucky ones in life-jackets,
drifting just out of reach, swallowed up by the sea,
bone-chilled, to be washed up on some distant shore.
Every one a neighbour, every one a neighbour's child.

Leila M.J
Ramesh
Azar Mohebbi Tehrani, Iranian singer

Although she was free, she decided not to sing, like all women in her
land. She died before seeing her country again, but she kept her return
ticket for forty-two years.

Kevin Qweaver Jackson
Soil music

Soil, the essence of us, finds its place,
makes a home, offers back
what it has, as it can. Moves
grain by grain, in as many ways
as there are songs to sing, recognising
no limits on its travels, except its own
requirements. But some,

suspicious of soil's freedoms, fence it in,
wall it off, impose rules of entry. And
from access controls, as lock follows key,
comes fear of loss, or disruption, or
any form of different. Thus fences get thicker,
walls higher. And all the time

soil becomes a little thinner, a little
less happy, a lot less nurturing.
And beneath the flowers
all manner of blades grow.

Cynthia Rodríguez Juárez
Ancestors Should be Exempt from Needing Passports

I find you, redhead,
suffocating and mimetic. Find you, shifting,
owl and lizard, snake, coyote. A creature
that branches into a family of human trees,
dodging bullets. Leaping through the Atlantic.

Ashen remains of Chichimecan rage transported,
needing documents, like Ozymandias needed
an Egyptian passport for antifungal treatment
in France. Turns out that borders leak
through the Afterlife.

You don't settle
for one animal, all genealogies are yours.
A shared imaginary of fire, independence
from the rising. Revolution from revolt.
An orange sliced by rains of arrows.

athina k
Settled Status App Fiasco

Remember the experience?
At Human Resources.
Putting your phone on your passport,
so it can be read.
Automation.
And a picture taken for facial recognition.
Your data is all theirs now, not yours.
Now you will be the European
settled in the UK.
Where they called out in the street shouting at you:
"Go back to your country asylum seeker."
Remember the experience.
Of your data, hostage for commercial use
And your soul registered and stored
by a government that definitely remains inhuman.

Orphée Kashala
Before I Die

I can see in the flames where the future lies
How it burns
How it hurts
And I cannot wait

I can see through the smoke what I cannot say
But I want nonetheless to take a chance today

To feel the warmth before the burn
To see the sun before it sets
To see the skies before it rains
To feel alive before I die

And if I make it out
I will not be the same
My scars alone will tell the tale
They'll show the world what I couldn't say
If you stitch it with gold
Is it worth the pain?

Margaret G. Kiernan
A House Against Itself

On paper some things look alike
Refuge into refugee, migrant into migrate
Man on bended knee at prayer
Or on a jugular vein
Brexit into black exit.

Pen your name, he said
But I can speak for me
Inflect my voice for your colonial interview
Smell the stench, like a corpsed grave
I know your game.

Not Notting Hill where the beats
Rap like Harlem on parade
I was good enough then, you loved cornbread
Left me to wash your dead, sat beside your sickly child
In the night shadows
When ghosts without colour
Drifted.

Leave to remain to mend those entrenched systems
That supported that man on bended knee
In whose name did he sign his work report, that day?
Yours? Mine? No not in my name.
Never

Rob Lowe
What Shall We Do

To be sung satirically to the tune of "What shall we do with the Drunken Sailor?", a 19ᵗʰ century sea shanty, in which each successive verse suggests a method of sobering or punishing the drunken sailor.

What shall we do with the homeless migrant?
How shall we deal with the homeless migrant?
Why should we love the helpless migrant?
Early in the dawn raid

Hooray, now we've caught her!
Hooray, now we've taught her!
Hooray, now we'll "ought" her
Early in the dawn raid

Put her in detention till she's homesick,
Put her in detention till she seems thick,
Put her in detention till she is sick
Early on the dawn raid

Put her in despair with the new laws round her,
Put her in despair till the new laws bind her,
Put her in despair till the new laws wound her
Early on the dawn raid

What shall we do with the seeking migrant?
What shall we do with her weeping children?
What shall we do with her needless wanting?
Early on the dawn raid

What is the world that we protect?
To keep the naked foreigner out;
What are the clothes we buy and wear?
What is this land we will not share?

Monica Manolachi
News From Timișoara

The merry-go-round giggles hysterically
in the middle of the new Iulius Town,
while the fairy-tale roofs of the cathedral
whisper softly about some martyrs of the past.
The birds flit from ramshackle mansions
to stylish restaurants and heavy prison gates,
walk among dandelions by the Bega River,
whilst the football stadium floodlights

warmly greet late yellow taxis –

They are all having a change of heart
whenever snow leopards come into town,
Naser and Ali, Hemat, Omar and Amir,
moving around like your brother,
determined and sly like your grandson,
adventurous like your cousin,
sensitive and clever like your lover,
hungry and worried like your son.

Carmina Masoliver
This Bitter British Winter

He has lived and worked here since he was twenty,
and hasn't seen his family in over a year now,
and though it will make his heart ache for them longer,
he begins the process to one day hold this own dark navy blue.

The first time he tells me he loves me, he's stressed with weekend work,
we are arguing over a cold Caribbean takeaway, and he wipes away my
tears.

He answers multiple choice questions on life
in the UK: Who is Queen Elizabeth II married to?
We've just passed St David's day and I didn't even know that,
or where the Cenotaph is, or who built the Tower of London.

That night, I practise the words in his ice-cold bathroom, and tell him
after our stomachs settle, slow and deliberate: seni seviyorum.

His family thousands of kilometres away, he has
thousands of pounds to pay for the Indefinite Leave to Remain
and then it turns into a twisted waiting game
where if it doesn't work, you try again and again.

The moon of his smile makes my sun shine;
we warm each other in this bitter British winter.

Gia Mawusi
Detritus

On the other side of the road
between the cracks in the walls
the moss grows,
unrestrained,
unbidden
free to feel,
to just be and subsist.
But on the edge of these bulwarks,
confined amidst these fences,
the gates of our living hell are tall
and we stand alone.

There is no safe haven across the Channel.
Just dreary buildings made of bricks and mortar,
unwelcoming our bodies
and crippling our souls.

And we hold up.
We hold on for that settlement letter
that will solve all
and make breathing,
living here
so much better.

Meanwhile,
the newspapers shout
for the world to believe,
point fingers at us
and see
just

leeches
whores
and thieves

detritus
undressed of humanity

adrift

Jenny Mitchell
Her Lost Language

English mouths are made of cloth,
stitched, pulled apart with every word.

Her life is mispronounced.
She cooks beef jollof rice for one;

braves the dark communal hall,
a giant's throat when he is lying down.

He's swallowed muffled voices,
stale breath of food and cigarettes.

The lift is shaped by urine.
The sky's a coffin lid.

Back in her village, days from Lagos,
hills take on the shape of God,

scant clouds the colour of her tongue.
Now she must walk past ghosts who leer like men,

to eat fast food from styrofoam,
binging to forget her scars

are less important every day,
when words must match

from one assessment to the next.
Back in her block, the lift vibrates

like an assault or panic rammed
beneath her skin by soldiers taking turns.

She Zooms to smile at parents
aging in their Sunday clothes.

They say more teachers have been raped.
A baobab tree is balanced on her father's head.

When the connection fails,
she flicks to channel *Save Yourself.*

A pastor bangs the podium, demands her *Hallelujah.*
She kneels to pray her papers will be stamped,

passport wrapped in green batik.
Pastor screams *Give thanks.*

Mehrzad Mohamadi
Tonight

I have left the city with its commotion
I have found peace in the desert

A mixture of zoze and stars and night
It tastes like the ice cream my mom made

The sun is slowly setting
The blue laughter of the sky

Turns to the silence of the red sun
The stars dance and come

Eyes, stars, sand in their magnificent dance
I and the moon are watching

I long for the rain of mercy
I watch for the first shoots of the pea

I have hidden my love under the soil of hope
I have hidden my love under the soil of hope

Hubert Moore
Leave to remain

Leave to remain is everything
and nothing. It's what you long for
but its small print doesn't
mention what you leave behind
when you remain.

Home smells, the lingering
of sounds. Some have to tell
themselves they'll never pass
their new-born child across
to grandparents to hold.

Every refugee has the story
of a refugee behind them.
How to leave your story,
leave the name of refugee
behind and be, happen

to be, a person who drives
taxis, a person watching swans
fly overhead, a person
whose first thought on waking
is of a sleeping child?

Hubert Moore
In the desert

Even at night your camels
knew the way across the desert
to the market where you sold
your latest load of mangoes.
We almost knew it too:
no lights, no road, no signposts,
only moon and stars and camel-sense
and like an undipped headlamp
your delighted expertise.

In UK after prison
then detention you found a place
in destitution, standing
only, in a telephone box
in Shepherd's Bush. Even this
was nothing to the eerie
desert in North London where
they found a room for you
which no one else would occupy.

Yasin Moradi
I come from

I come from a warm city with many mountains
I ended up with a cold city without any mountains

I come from dust
Finally, I'll return to the dust

I come from a city with brutal police
I ended up with Home Office

I come from a crossing sea
To find a place with peace

Cheryl Moskowitz
Asylum

I ask you about home
and you tell me
that home is where the river runs,
home is where the dates grow
in bunches
and dry, brown in the sun.
Home is where your father
farms the land and drives his horses.
Home is where you have a father,
or did have.

I ask you where you come from
and you say
I come from here
Here is where you're from,
no back story,
no foreigner's tale
because only strangers are foreign -
and you are not strange,
you are human
like me.

You ask me
how I spend my days
and my nights
and I tell you that I spend my days thinking,
and my nights writing poetry in a dark place
so I can try to imagine
what it might be like
to leave a prison behind in one country
only to arrive in another
the next.
You ask me about home
and I tell you.

Cheryl Moskowitz
This is a letter to you

You do not know me, or my country, but I know your son,
so let me begin by telling you he is here, alive, safe, of
course I do not mean unscarred, I do not mean undamaged,
I do not mean he lives without fear or pain, or that he is not
missing what he can't ever have back, you, his childhood,
he tells me how grateful he is, asks for my blessing, out of
respect he says, the way a child shows appreciation to a
parent, though I am not – but you are, you are his mother
and he carries you in tattoos and dreams, in what he
cannot remember, is not allowed to tell, things you could
not save him from, don't cry, he is happy, though
nightmares make him sleepless, afraid, but do not cry, your
son is here and he tells me that he loves you.

I do not know this man he calls Uncle, who came from your
husband's village, your trust was too easily given, forgive
me, he was no uncle, though he took what you had as if it
was his, your house, your food, your children, he knew you
were good people, not the sort to look over their shoulder
with suspicion, or cast someone out when he's hungry,
your son, he could see, was impressionable, he knew a boy
like that, good, bright, 7 years old, would take the hand of
an uncle like him, he knew with your blessing, your son
would obey, touch his feet, touch him, he assured you that
even when you were not there, then he, Uncle, would take
care of everything, and you, grateful, placed your hand on
his head and gave him your blessing.

We need to have people we call *our* people, people we can trust, no one is blaming you for that, especially not your son who remembers each day how good you were, how you taught him the importance of manners and how even when you are unwell you should be well-groomed, and he remembers the rules you set and how when he wanted money for cigarettes and knives, you said you would give him something to save his life instead, pressed his head gently under water and taught him to swim, skills are for life you said, no one can take learning from you, and you were right, though you could not know, how this Uncle in your house was intent on taking everything, the gift you gave your son of life and manners and staying afloat.

You are not here to see him, but I tell him I know you and he bends and touches my feet and asks me to bless him as your son and I tell him you are happy and safe and proud to hear that he still practices when he can at the YMCA, and that no harm ever came, even after he left, when you helped him to leave, even after Uncle returned with those bad men on bikes, with their knives and black smoke, he cuts himself sometimes, to *bleed away pain*, afraid what was done to him might cause harm to you, he is a good boy, and alive, unlike you, so I tell him that you and I are friends, share secrets with one another like sisters, and I tell him, that one day God willing, you will come to see him in this city and watch him while he swims.

Loraine Masiya Mponela

Do not give me Indefinite Leave to Remain when I have lost my mental capacity

Do not give me Indefinite Leave to Remain
When I have lost my mental capacity.

What does it take
For me to qualify as a good immigrant?
Good at what?
Am I not good enough as I am?

Is it education?
How about my Masters degree?
Is it volunteering?
I have lost count of my voluntary work.

Is it leadership and participation?
I have the trust of my community and led for many years.
Is it good character?
According to which assessor?

Is it awards?
Well, I've stopped counting,
From everyday hero
To, now, modern day Lady Godiva.

What is it?
Aren't we humans first?
Why are you blind to see what's wrong with the system?
Mandela, Gandhi, Rosa Parks, were their lives in vain?
Is Marcus Rashford also wrong?

Freedom is nowhere near.
You go through torture to get food.
Families are torn apart
Scattered in the land of isolation.

Do not give me Indefinite Leave to Remain
When I have lost my mental capacity.
How will I find the sanity to recognize it
Or to use or appreciate it?

Life has lost meaning.
In fact, end it now
If this is what makes your life easier
So I can no longer be a drain to your economy.

I have had enough of your torture,
Torment and mental foul play.
Let me go.
If I don't go now, end it all now.

Do not give me Indefinite Leave to Remain
When I have lost my mental capacity.
I will no longer see it as a gift.
I will not be able to show my gratitude.

A large part of me will be dead
And I die every day I am denied.
Do not give me Indefinite Leave to Remain
When I have lost my mental capacity.

Loraine Masiya Mponela
Do not let Bukhary be forgotten

Today, 18 July 2021
Is another dark day
Another death in asylum hotel
Another body without a soul
Bukhary Afifi Ahmad
Is no more

A young Sudanese asylum seeker
So far away from home
Confronted by a hostile system
Living in poor conditions and neglect
Suffering from the never ceasing trauma
Of war, death and destruction

A man who has never known peace
Concerns were raised but ignored
It becomes too much
Echoes of loneliness
Change to echoes of pain

Now we are left with questions

Why Bukhary, why
Without disclosing even to one friend?
How many emergency demonstrations will it take
To stop these deaths?
Do we wait for them
And regroup again and ask, Why?

Do not let Bukhary be forgotten

Loraine Masiya Mponela
Penny Walker

Penny   you gave us a tranquil place filled with love and care   taking
away our homeless and shame   clothing us   giving us a place to call
home

The home you gave us is a peace garden where   just like us   all plants
grow   there's a Zimbabwean cabbage and rhubarb that endure all
weather   they never change   green   peace and love all year round   never
dying like your love   a garden of peace with creeping strawberries ready
for the picking   creeping beans ready for harvest   every fruit and plant
special like the touch of your hands   standing plants that give birth to
sweet fruits pregnant with aroma that even babies can pick   a symbol to
how accessible you were

Penny   your love grows like the cherry tomatoes and big tomatoes
growing side by side with sunflowers   yellow flowers bringing light like
the love you gave

You left us a foodbank house with two apple trees standing majestically
at the back and another in front which bear green and red apples   a mix
of sweet and sour that fall freely to the ground like your tears at the sight
of the homeless   you left us a home that we now share with many visitors
including the birds that make their presence known in loud song and the
mess they leave on our table

You left us a calming sanctuary   a garden of yellow roses and white
flowers that shine as bright as the full moon at night   where I sit and at
times play football or dance to my tribal healing songs   I remember you
always when I sit in this hotspot where I walk barefoot connecting my
body with nature   grounding   feeling the warmth under my feet   peace
garden   a place where we can rest from the sun's penetrating rays   a place

where we can light open fires and feel the warmth rise from the feet to the crown of our heads   here I burn away my struggles and calm my mind

Penny Walker (23 October 1950 - 21 May 2021) was an "extraordinary campaigner for non-violence, sustainability and peace in South Warwickshire, Coventry and Leicester" (Richard Johnson, *Independent Catholic News*, 26 May 2021). For more on the truly exemplary life Penny led, see: https://www.indcatholicnews.com/news/42287

Ambrose Musiyiwa
Martians, Effing Martians

Shall we blame Martians
for everything that is wrong
with the world?
Shall we scan every building
every meeting
living
breathing
space
for signs of Martians?
Shall we prod Earthlings
ask them to be on guard
and report
round up
or bash
any Martian
sighted
or imagined?
Shall we bring out spaceships
and start patrolling the streets?
Shall we fit PA systems to the spaceships
and play messages on a loop
telling Martians to go back home
that if they do not leave voluntarily
we will come for them
and forcibly remove them?
Shall we round up all Martians
put them in detention centres
put them on the next spaceship to Mars?
Shall we gas them?
Shall we nuke them?

Chad Norman
The Lighting of a Candle

It stands before me
still unlit
unlike the spreading problem
lit over & over because of hatred,
or am I wrong, am I afraid,
hatred is no fool, hatred is,
and I am not wrong or afraid
when it comes to what my pen wants.

I don't give a damn about keyboards,
or computers or cellphones, or that
unbelievable mouth called Social Media,
I give a damn about my country,
one known as Canada, one worth
giving more than a damn about, one,
the only one I have to give myself to.

The lighting of a candle
now bright, now lit long ago,
well maybe not so long ago
if I put aside any belief in time,
how it seems to be mad to pass,
to leave us another confusion as to
why it passes by day after day
in such an inexplicable hurry.

Please understand our world is not small,
meaning there is room, so much room
for one family, all the families who need
to escape what they call danger, what
we would call a report on the nightly news,
what I need to call an invitation,
"Please come to my country, you know
it is known as Canada, so many have come
before you, families, children, man & woman,
who stand somewhere with one match, with
one ancient and simple faith,
the lighting of a candle
can be a beginning, can be
like when a child is newly born
and the world becomes borderless,
the world is found in each & every flicker."

Sarah Nymanhall
For The Children's Sake

How did you do it?
You know – gather your guts together
Pack up the lives you knew and leave
the country of your birth to grieve for
your remembered history in that place
This will always be your mystery
that I never solve, because I'll
never meet you face to face or
hear your answer from the grave
yet I marvel at your bravery and
how it is to leave so much behind
Your friends your home your village
your country your life as you know it

Tears in your eyes and pain in your heart
Souls shrivelled by fear but you can't show it
For the children's sake you must stand tall
For the children's sake you must look strong
even in those fleeting moments when
you wonder if you've made the wrong choice
that could tear your family's life apart
yet when your children start to cry
you make yourself remember
why it is you have to leave and
so you grieve in secret and in silence
It is an all embracing family affair
Not one member left there to perish or yearn
It is a journey of no return

You keep your sense of home afloat
by everyone boarding the boat to somewhere
Nothing but sea and sky to stare into
Your skin stung by the salt filled air

Who knows how you ended up in Leeds
where tall brick chimneys belched forth
thick smoke that darkened even the
sky of a summer's day

But who cares – you got away –
Nourished your hope to create a new home
in a place that at first felt unknown

I speak to you as a child from that hoped for future
since you are a precious part of my own history

Denise O'Hagan
The Quiet Assimilators

Take almost any street, in any modern city
And we are there. We are the substrata
        of society
Ever-present, the unseen lining, the padding
In the crowd. We carry our backgrounds
Closer than our wallets, effortlessly
Yet they inform our every step, invisibly.

Because unlike our children, if we have them,
We were not born in this country we call home
Shook off the reassuring, cloying familial ties
Jumped through immigration hoops,
        applied for
Visas and lingered in alien passport queues
Later sealing our legitimacy in citizenship status
And all the while, getting used to new ways
Of doing things.

We have assimilated, oh God
        have we assimilated
Tailoring ourselves to blend in how we dress,
Our turns of speech, its intonation,
        and countless
Other ways, or so we let ourselves believe until
A chance remark, "And where is *your* accent
        from?"
Undoes us in a second.

So we try just that bit harder, and encourage
        our children,
If we have them, just that bit more. The big
        divide, you see,
Never was the traditional culprits of language
        or religion
(we've heard it all before), but this: that
        we take nothing
For granted.

Yet a kernel of obstinance buds and grows
        inside us
And we feel, unaccountably and frustratingly,
Growing closer to the land we left behind,
        acquiring
A latent faithfulness to old ways, rituals
        and rhythms
Which fix themselves, like beacons in
        our penumbral minds,
The way we left them years, decades perhaps, ago.

And so the circle closes, leaving us
Respectable citizens of the establishment
Outside, but wavering inside, daring
In our weaker moments, to wonder
If we ever should have come.

Catherine Okoronkwo
aliens live

in cafes watching dressed-up people drinking mochas
beneath shop windows displaying anorexic mannequins
on circular bus travelling from Perry Barr to Acocks Green
at Heartlands Hospital waiting for bloods to be taken and meds given

in dreams where *ndị nna nna* reveal glimpses of a world beyond
days wrapped in church sale coats two sizes too big
bunioned toes in ill-fitting shoes kicking up damp autumn leaves
scavenging commercial bins for half-eaten or out-of-date food

hidden behind a shed, unable to sleep, a fox chases a squirrel
in the darkness, tears stream at lost years, exhausted dreams, handcuffed
by Home Office robots. I once read in a Chinese fortune cookie,
"aliens live in a small village on the edge of the Arctic Circle".

David Owen
Pieta

The child is settled in his father's arms.
Held rocky-steady even as parental eyes
Jitter nervously over inked in papers
Seeking "leave to remain".
Such an odd phrase, he thinks, as if
You must go away to come back and stay.
The child stirs a little, shift-wriggles, until
His dad's voice settles him once more.
The flat is clean but damp leaks through walls
And there are the signs of daily battle
Against defects: brushes, bucket, cloth rags.
Pride confronts fate. To be endured.
He'd been an engineer before the soldiers came.
He'd designed offices. Sun-touched towers
That became bomb-sculptures,
Steel girders twisting out of concrete
As cries of abstracted anguish.
The child is waking.
He banishes memory and smiles down
At his son – their status is settled,
They are all each has left that remains.

S. Muge Ozbay
What Remains

I touch my bones
To find the strength of my ancestors.
I breathe
To create space for my heart.
What remains
When everything that made you is lost.
Does one have to forget everything?
Sometimes, out of the blue, the remembrance
Of the smell of toasted bread for breakfast
And the laid-back hug of a lover
Fill me with the sensation of being at home,
That welcoming feeling of the simple flow of days.

Evicted, homeless, a husk of myself,
A walker in the streets,
Starving, but light.
Lightheaded,
I evaporate into the city,
Diffuse like light.
Walking, I kiss the earth
And the pavements with light feet.
I touch this land lightly,
Like a shadow.
My body becomes the streets and forests of London.
The ground we share,
The ground to rise and stand.
And there is always the sky.

The more shed, the more found.
And something passes through me.
No language belongs to me
And I belong to no land.
Only the sea and the rivers.
What passes through me arrives home
Only when I am immersed
In the earth's waters.
And there is always the sky.

Nasrin Parvaz
The price of "freedom"

Going away the day you're
given your passport,
as if you found wings
to escape from an arranged marriage.
The passport officer smiles,
"It seems you didn't have a nice time here."
You smile back.

You don't go back
to the life you once had,
but to a new self
into the anonymity of the world,
exiled from exile.

Pascale Petit
Passport

I sew leaves together for the passport,
a slug trails the finest mirror-writing.

And the watermark? Printed by an ocean.

At the border an owl stamps
my passport with his claw.

Only he can see the pages fall
every winter, regrow each spring.

My passport is round
but there are those
who still believe it's flat,

that an ant will sail off the edge
into the vacuum of an airport terminal.

My biometric fingerprints
have a scent only a jackal can read.

A woodpecker types me
a residence permit
from his high office,

but still no word from the government.
Will they send me that verdict –
prepare to leave our kingdom!

Home Office –
I am a citizen of the wild,
my address is a cloud,

my date of birth
the innermost ring of earth's crust.

And the country of my birth?

Have you heard the chants
of the snowy tree crickets?

One enters my room like a violinist
from a far galaxy,
who knows how to sing
the word "foreigner" in my language

until the whole house
trills with his kyrie eleison –

Lord, have mercy on strangers.

Stephanie Powell
Passenger

another country
a ballad of street signs in a foreign tongue
a sandstorm drops over the metropolis
bike bells ring through the dust-fog
underground cables stretch all the way to a cold shore
the other way to humid sea
the ferryman watches the high-rises grow nearer, more ropes,
more pylons, more pipelines
everything pulling forward to the collapse of water
a hundred-foot woman dances over a crowded square
light spills over the strip clubs, fast food spots, department stores
the arms-length away feeling of a plane sinking over a new city
the endless track of airport travelators
midnight in transit
descending over fair valley, quiet country, another field,
another apartment block
another storm birthing over landfall
another visitor:

looking into passing faces for a map-
setting out on unsure earth.

Jova Bagioli Reyes
A Letter to Little Amal

My how your feet must bleed
Splitting blistered seams on the rocks
How your dreams must be weaving in and out of
splattering with which we write on the wall
"Refugees Welcome"

Now that you are here
And have been welcomed with open arms
I have so many questions for you

Did you leave Aleppo in ruins?
Do you remember what it was like before?
What image do you have of home?
The one they gave you or the one they stole?

Did you pass by Rojava on your way?
Did Erdogan bless you as he cursed the Kurdish anarchists?
Did you pass by Armenia and witness a centennial of genocide?

Did you circumvent Palestine?
Did you know the IDF would strip you apart?
Were you afraid they would burn you like the olive trees?

Did you pass through Moria into open borders?
Did you smell the ashes and hear the silence
Heavy on the ears of those who are left?

Did you look out into the Mediterranean
Did you look at the waves and realize
That they were but bodies?
Did they offer you food and water
on the docks of Bari instead of spit?
Did they call you an art piece instead of a problem?

Did you pass through Calais?
Did you wait years just to be heard?
Did it ever get easier?

How did you pass through so easily?
When so many could not
When Europe is dressed in barbed wire
and the moat is filled with gunboats
and Britain washes its hands with nice words at teatime
and the sun has not set for a while
and fast fash is in fashion
and every day there are more eyes on you
hands on you
and words in your mouth that you did not put there

and all you can do is stare incredulously
at those who would justify this

Who here would welcome you if you were not wooden?
Who here would applaud you if you were a grown woman?
Who here would bless you if you were hijabi?
If you were bearded?
If you were angry?
If you could speak?

My how your dreams must bleed
When you finally fall asleep

This poem was written in response to *The Walk*, a performance piece centred around Little Amal, a 9-year-old Syrian refugee child character from *The Jungle* (Faber and Faber, 2018), a play by Joe Murphy and Joe Robertson. For *The Walk*, Little Amal was turned into a 3.5 meter-tall puppet and walked from the Syrian-Turkish border, through Europe, until reaching Manchester, UK, where Jova performed their poem. While the performance included various acts that symbolically welcomed Little Amal to the city, Jova wanted to highlight the injustice and hypocrisy that refugees face every day as well as the conditions that forced them to flee their homes in the first place.

Kay Ritchie
removed

like a package stamped and posted off
return to sender scrawled in red
it starts with a bang on the door in the night
the fright as you're mishandled bundled
tossed into a van
no *fragile* pasted to your front
just demands for documentation
you're labelled now
you've overstayed
no longer welcome here
go home
immigration
isolation
no communication
or information
till deportation
and like an international airmail
you're folded into a flight
to who knows where
arriving in some cargo bay
far away
on your own
address unknown
trying to start again

Richard Roe
Mohammad, My Friend

Mohammad was sitting on a bench when we last met.
He smiled as he always did. I was welcome.
We talked generalities as always.
Our friendship is real.
His need is real.
He knows I care.
He knows I want to help.
His challenges are too great for him to live the life he deserves.
I cannot help.
He knows I cannot help.
He is grateful that I care.
We talk generalities.
He lives in my heart.

I met and befriended Mohammad at the Coventry Refugee and Migrant Centre (CRMC). I knew him for about two years. He was a lovely gentle giant of a man, but had been attacked and suffered brain damage. He lived and died on the streets of Coventry. When his body was discovered between two buildings, it had been there months and took three months through DNA tests matching relatives from Africa to identify the body. CRMC organised the funeral.

Caroline Rooney
The Key Workers

The nurses who gave me my vaccine
were Asian; the man I think Indian
and the woman probably Japanese.

That time I was operated on
and nearly died, the nurse by my side
all night was from an African country.

The driver who has been delivering
my groceries this isolated year
is called Mohammed, not sure from where.

The guys who run the neighbourhood shops
are Turkish, Bulgarian, Indian.
I myself am resident alien.

Priti Patel, you said to protect
our public services *vote to leave*
because immigrants overwhelm us.

K J Rowswell
Missing from Class

You came into my class to learn English
While you waited
For permission to stay.
For it was to live and work
In England
That you journeyed all this way.

I saw both fear and hope in your eyes,
The sadness of loss pushed back
As you dare to smile.
The courage which brought you so far
Now daring to hope
That all pain and all loss would be worthwhile.

Loss of home, culture, family, friends,
Of the self you seek the freedom to be
Away from oppression's lie.
The pain of your parting cuts deep
With every border you cross, as further
From all you hold dear you fly.

But today you were not in my class.
Only a note of permission withheld
For you to settle here.
So your journey for freedom continues
As you seek a place to be
And the right to live without fear.

Burak Sahin
Mr Nobody

Mr Nobody feels under the weather most of the time. He moved all the way from sunny lands to dark shores with a dream. Even though the people he saw when he arrived at this new land were lovely and seemed interesting, he never felt he belonged. He does not belong where he came from. He does not belong to this land either. *Where is home?* he thinks. He heard something new from a wise man, who said, Time flies. So it did. While time passed, he forgot what his dreams were, where his home was. He forgot what his name was. Thus, he became Mr Nobody, just trying to save the day in his little room, making circles.

Barbara Saunders
To Aleppo Gone

a small grey boy on an orange seat
rubs a hand over an eye to see why
it runs, he doesn't cry
he smears something, red dust
a sudden beat of concrete
the law of entropy when homes fall
a pile he's pulled from
to sleep, to be re-born
in the silence of a small, red brain
that digs itself beneath
a small grey boy
patched, dispatched
to an orange seat
last seen in the media
waiting, waiting, how long?

Maggie Sawkins
Teaching English at Friendship House

Although he came from the mountains
this much I learnt

he didn't understand my words
for snow.

I fluttered my fingers
in front of him

but he only saw
the wings of birds.

I led him to the window
wrapped myself in my arms

at the shivering sky
but he only stared.

It was slow and involved
the elimination

of sun, wind and rain
but we got there.

Sometimes I think of him
back at the border

I imagine his mountains
their fingers of shadow

the stutter of gunfire
the quietness of snow.

Ian Seed
Rome

Early each morning in the eternal city, I carried a knotted handkerchief full of sand so that I could feel its weight in my palm. In this way, I wouldn't forget where I'd come from. But then I'd pour the sand onto the pavement to remind myself I was free each morning to choose my life anew.

With my empty handkerchief back in my pocket, I would go to the café on the corner for a black coffee. There was never anyone in there at that time, apart from the owner and his wife, neither of whom seemed in a hurry to serve me.

Naledi Segosebe
Settled Status for All

i say we settle this
once and for all
a change of status
to settled
for all
fresh start
for all

let charity have a chance
to begin here
at home
let's share it in tons
with all here
or will we sever our own nose
wholly to spite our own face?

i say we wipe the slate clean

has history taught us nothing?

the only way out is together
this ungodly split will get us undone
it brings out what we can't defend

i say we resolve this right now
fair access to resources
will result in wellness
for all

Suzan Criscentia Spence
Mercy

Her story disappeared from the headline news
"A woman in Glasgow starved herself to death"
Another asylum seeker with nothing left to lose.

A callous rejection removed her right to choose,
so she stayed indoors at a temporary address.
Her story disappeared from the headline news.

They didn't believe her and she couldn't prove it,
as she spoke of her life and wasted her breath
Another asylum seeker with nothing left to lose.

She was not wanted. They did not approve.
It was stalemate in a game of suicide chess.
Her story disappeared from the headline news.

Desperation fed neglect and self-abuse.
How did this happen? They could only guess.
Another asylum seeker with nothing left to lose?

Glasgow had a whip-round to bury their communal shame
Spoke kind words for Mercy Baguma, said no one was to blame.
Her story disappeared from the headline news
Another asylum seeker with nothing left to lose.

Paul Stephenson
The Danish Vote

came as weary leaders called to seal the
borders of the Balkans, the foothills of
the Carpathians and shores of the
Dalmatians. Under new laws, they seized
the corners of every foreign field, the
brambly brims and crinkle-cut brinks
where year on year, young couples had
been betrothed. Armies soon rounded up
the lower bourns and closest contours.
They took diameters, deep dividing lines,
the easternmost edges where exhausted
enemies had ceased the fire, happy to get
their hands on natural depressions and
elevations, glad to enclose enclaves and
grant no stays. How they cracked down
hard on extremities where young
children were buried, expropriated the
flanks and frontiers, blocked the
gateways to graveyards. Only gusts
remained. Skirting highest hems, police
arrested the hawthorn hedges,
impounded islands and distant
isthmuses, grabbed the jaggedy bits
jutting out, cutting them off completely.
They occupied outermost reaches,
arrested picket fences, pillaging the
porous periphery, reducing it to a
powder. Over-running ravines and quartz
quarries, they took A-roads and B-roads,
left well alone the rusting lorries.
Settlements were sequestered at the
tailend of nowhere, not to mention

thalwegs, thresholds, tombolos; wherever the old tribe survived. They uncovered the underbelly of umpteen verges, built a vast wall to silence the waterfall, locked emergency exits to the feint margin of peace over yonder.

In January 2016, Denmark enacted a new law allowing police to seize refugees' assets

Diliana Stoyanova
We're here

Travelers, aliens, wanderers,
strangers, refugees, foreigners,
outsiders,
survivors,
we're here.

A raceless, landless, disconnected tribe
held together by Whatsapp and Skype,
family trees and friendships growing on Facebook ground
relationships where picture doesn't always synch with sound;
having all the time zones see just a corner of your room,
as we might be in lockdown but you spit out fire spoken word on Zoom,
we're here.

"When was the last time you went home?" you ask. Oh dear.
We go home every night and haven't been home in years.
Home is an airport bench, a coffee shop with good wi-fi,
home is the ragged breath we take after every goodbye,
home is 23 kilos in a rolling suitcase,
not a house but a moment, and a breathing space.
Home is where we are in or out of place,
home is an instant of human connection that we embrace;
we're here.

We speak one too many languages and none are fluent.
"One more alphabet won't hurt", yeah that was stupid.
And yes, we have used a dictionary at the shop
because last time we got sugar instead of salt.
And business cards because we are sick of spelling our names
(and of course I mean those that aren't Sam, John or James).

And every time we pronounce things wrong or make a mistake
we feel so so stupid, like for fuck's fucking sake.
We translate, we search for the words and the grammar,
we translate ourselves and our souls and sometimes we stammer.
But we try, again and again and again despite feeling rejected
because all that we want is to be understood. And accepted.
We're here

Every day we wear our organs on the outside,
'cause the insides of our bodies are occupied
by different words for the exact same things.
But there's the exact same humanity
right underneath our skins.
We're here.

The rootless, the tongue-less, the restless,
The helpless, the aimless, the reckless
The outcast, the voiceless, the faithless,
The exiled, the faceless, the state-less
The immigrants
The differents.

We are right here.

Marie-Therese Taylor
Citizenship Test
Letter to accompany an application for asylum
from the head of the family with whom the applicant is staying

Sir, I know this boy.
He fled when they burned his home in the mountains
southeast of Turkey.

He still walks the ridge
where guards made their mark
on his twelve year old thigh.

He stopped his ears
as the soldiers entered
his nine year old sister.

This boy has watched
the sunset on pity
and there is no beauty.

What is it, you ask,
that language he speaks?
(Your question is heavy).

How many can he?
Only the one, only his own
learned from his mother

and the songs of strangers
round half-mended walls
of unwelcome tents

as he crossed unmarked
unmarked borders
of indifferent states.

You say, he must learn ours
if he wants to live here.
Yet he already has

thirty or more
names for the wind.
He never translates.

When you talk of his flight
please think about birds
– their costly migration

the strength of their hope
the weight of their wings
and the sigh of their landing.

Angela Topping
The Dispossessed

Shamima, why did you go?
Stole your sister's passport,
plotting with your friends
to leave behind the humdrum.
The lure to be grown-up,
marriage and motherhood, choosing
a niqab over school uniform,
for a bundle of wild promises.
What did they say to make you
believe you'd be better off?
Your two friends are dead,
your children had no future.
How can you begin
to come to terms with that?
All you had left was the rag
of your British citizenship,
now stripped away against the law.
Stateless, childless, separated
from the husband chosen for you.
I wish for you a clean page,
a rebirth, the chance to explain,
start a normal life, away from
those who would exploit you,
a new understanding of the world.

Lauren Tormey
Temporary

I am not temporary
But that's the label you put on me
You tell me that 8 years and 6 months is temporary
But 9 years and I'm suddenly permanent

A global crisis isn't happening at 9 years
It's happening at 8 years and 6 months
If I lose my job you won't help me
If I lose my job I can't meet your income requirement
If I lose my job you won't make me permanent

Why
I met your stupid requirements this whole time
I never asked for help this whole time
Why does 6 months from the finish line make me less deserving of security
Hell, why should 6 years make me less deserving

Your arbitrary rules and timelines force me into a state of needless anxiety
You've made a choice to make me feel this way
To make every immigrant feel this way
Some of them aren't living in a state of 'if' though
They're suffering and you just stand by and let them
All because you choose to define our existence as temporary

I am not temporary
I am not permanent either
I just am
We all just are

Ursula Troche
This Land

Here I am, with my
sordid status symbol, settled
status, now set in my place
and this land that isn't mine

this land is your land,
it isn't my land, in Cumbria
and all over the island
from the Epping Forest
to the North Sea Waters
this land wasn't made for
all of us,

especially not foreigners
though some of us got status
to stay, that's so unsettling, it
creates a line between us
another border, more division

meanwhile what
is the status of our stories?
what do they mean
in this country that's not mine
with an unsettled state of mind.

Lytisha Tunbridge
Ask Yourself

Exiled, with no hope
Crept out of camp
Fled our lands
Are you hallucinating?

Crept out of camp
Intermittent food and water
Are you hallucinating
Looking for the promises

Intermittent food and water
Once we had a community
Looking for the promises
Rocks jag our feet

Once we had a community
Fled our lands
Rocks jag our feet
Exiled, with no hope

Deborah Tyler-Bennett
Your Side of the Pond

Imagine, if you will, stretch of water
nearby where you live (river, lake, canal)
wide-stretch, perhaps wider than it looks,
overhung by willow and the usual, nameless, weeds.
Somewhere walked most days alone, or with
partner … children … dog …
Just think, the further bank's identical as that
you stroll by, but the land's different jurisdiction.

Most days they're seen, shadow figures
gazing at where you stand –
sometimes you raise a hand
in greeting – often not.

Imagine, today, coming across them at the water's edge
face down where rushes shade
young man and little girl (could have been his daughter)
you knew them dead, as treescapes blurred.
Groping to call someone, another watcher
on your side, had seen them too
walked up, and hand upon your shoulder cried:
"Oh Christ, what did we do?"

PR Walker
Closer to Calais

I've read about the nightly game of chicken
on the motorway, forcing lorries heading
for the tunnel to slow just enough for others
to lift a strapped load, climb aboard unseen.
I've read about the ones who don't make it
in freezer units, clinging to undercarriages,
the straits that foster such craving, the fear
of always being the wrong side of the water.

I'm tunnel bound. Half an hour out I stop
for a tank of cheap diesel. At the pump,
I glance in the rear-view mirror and see
six anxious faces rise from a hidden ditch,
watch as they recce, then sprint towards
rows of parked-up trucks – two Waberers,
an Eddie Stobart are options among them.

As I return from the pay-station key in hand,
a slow, disconsolate retreat is underway.
A face breaks ranks and moves towards me,
eyes fixed on mine, hands a gesture of prayer.
Take me to England in the boot of your car,
I hesitate, activate the remote. The eyes plead.
I know my luggage space is return-trip empty.

Gail Webb
Undocumented

Arriving in the back of a van
parked up on the A46
is not the best introduction,
not the welcome she was promised.

Doors flung open, the cold air hits
taking her breath away, slapping
her hopes of a warm welcome
hard against frozen tarmac.

On the long journey here, pressed up
against strangers, she was dreaming
of her new life, a room of her own,
time to study, to make friends.

Inside the lorry it is so dark,
cars are rushing by fast, dodging
bodies darting across the road,
disappearing into woods.

She is not quick enough, turns out,
her feet stick to damp grass verges
trapping her there, police arrive
lights flashing blue in her pupils.

No identity papers, none,
she feels no need, no one knows her
either here or in her far away home,
just a girl to be exploited.

One week later she tries hard
to tell authorities of hell, torture,
the life she had before she came,
her hopes to be just a girl here.

Is anyone listening? She watches,
sees pens moving, checking boxes;
being processed makes her feel lifeless,
her only hope to escape, run again.

Patricia Welles
souvenirs

drizzle storm in a westminster teacup
overflowing with pain london rain
flushing into eyes a toilet of despair
refugees hide in arches of a palace
lie beneath a history of bridges
attend their own funerals
when no one is looking
they bury their dead in parks
where acres of gardens white and ginger flowers
dot an ancient landscape
simple wishes – food – a shower – unblocking loos
against Pistorius assault are unheeded
no love on this horizon nothing
only dark intentions lies inventions
hiding the sick the dying
toilet paper coffins for the unwanted
while tourists light a candle in the abbey
for their departed then buy souvenirs

Richard Williams
The Transmutation of Geese

They're out on the sand-spits,
the marshlands and mudflats,
the in-between ground,
where shapes shift in the half-life;
a sliver of nearly-made earth.

Aristotle believed
six thousand miles from autumn
was a distance beyond all sense,
so birds would change with seasons,
one species to another.

Is this the way of all migrants,
to live life at the borders
not quite out of sight,
and in the minds of unbelievers
to be what they are not?

Kimmika L. H. Williams-Witherspoon
Customs

Why is it that the Black woman
Monied mother, Professor
with handsome, young son
freshly flung from all night flight across "the pond"
all-nighter-tired; but, "pressing on"
anticipation mounting, anxious & excited
new journey
Heathrow – Customs, crowded
with others, claiming capital, currency, privilege or both.
Why is it *always* Black Bodies,
Scrutinized the hardest, delayed,
Privileged by ritual acts of power
Meant, to dehumanize & discourage.
Why is it always *us*
holding up the line
held to a separate standard
a separate time –
separate symbol to the sign
while uniformed officials
play out the unequal ritual
performances of monied man versus
Black woman, Professor Who *can* –
But only under certain conditions.
Can't ever forget to remember
Sadly – "used" to it –
It's always one or the other –
either criminalizing *Black*
or making invisible.

Kimmika L. H. Williams-Witherspoon
Acculturation

Long ago She would have been at home
Way back when, down home – African
Whether East, West, Southern Saharan or Nubian
Skin moist and smooth
Shiny in the noon day sun.
One of the many who would have –
Foraged for food
Manned the pots
Used pestle and stone
Pound flour from grain.

And then the white people came
& everything changed –
Carnage, Conquest, Christianity,
Colonialism. Commodification,
Chattel slavery,
Cultural imperialism,
Capitalism.

Today. Once subject of the crown
She rides the tube
Pushing carriage with plump, dark baby
Wrapped up well against the cold.
A bracelet of beads about her wrist –
Reminders of home
Braids so tight
"Her kitchen"
Like a foyer!
Skin moist and smooth
Shiny in the noon day sun

With her cultural memory, seemingly, undone –
Generations removed from who
We once were,
African woman
With Black baby in carriage
Riding tube through city streets foreign
Balancing life & a time's history full of
Carnage – generations of dislocation –
Carrying a host of backpack images,
Like worms to the mind,
Proudly sporting every *white* Disney princess
That generational self-hate
Can find.

Michele Witthaus
What Was Left Behind

The last time I saw my father
he was helping me leave in haste.
Carrying my bag downstairs
he stopped on the landing
to catch his breath
and I saw how old I had made him.
His brow was laced with lines
that looked to me like anger
and I wished I had not
shared the burden
of my lawyer's question:
How soon can you go?

Michele Witthaus
Home Affairs

Liverpool sent me to Croydon
but Croydon would not let me in.
Did not care to know why I'd come:
Different department, they said.

I sent myself back to Watford,
in a bid to work out what was wrong;
spread out the patchwork of papers
I'd put all my details on.

Liverpool gave me a deadline so close
I could not help but default.
Croydon advised I ignore it:
Different department, they said.

Liverpool wrote me a letter,
warning I might have to go
back to a place they referred to as home
but not saying where that might be.

I'd just about given up when, one day,
a different department – again! –
confirmed, without warning, in triplicate,
Indefinite Leave to Remain.

Michele Witthaus
When My Cover is Blown

I pass unnoticed until I speak,
then strangers start to guess.
'Australia!' they venture.
I shake my head politely;
wait as they hazard New Zealand.
I'm British, I say at last.
I have no need to justify
my circuitous route to this place.
But where are you *from*?
they ask, undeterred.
And I wonder, do they mean:
Why did you come?
Who let you in?
How dare you think
that you belong?

Gregory Woods
The Evidence of Things Not Seen

1

Kampala

Discretion was his only scant
Asylum from hostility.
For fear of being beaten, he
Concealed the truth about himself,
Defensively unclubbable.
Policing gesture, gait and tone
Of voice, he made a habit of
Performance, always speaking lines
He'd learned by rote, if not by heart,
Avoiding being judged as what
Society would not condone.
The evident is not the self.

2

London

But now the apparatchiks of
Identity require him to
Be more identifiable:
A fluent wrist, a swish, a lisp,
A love of Broadway musicals –
Whatever, short of bodily
Corroboration on the desk,
Might constitute defining proof.
Their unresponsive faculties,
Insensitive to nuance, fail
To register a simple truth:
The self is not self-evident.

Mantz Yorke
No Trivial Pursuit

*To naturalise and become a citizen of the UK, you must be over 18 years
old, be of "good character", be currently living in the UK, meet English
language requirements, and pass the Life in the UK test.*

I didn't know
how many members make up the Northern Ireland Assembly;
how often its Welsh equivalent holds elections;
the Scottish clan slaughtered for refusing to swear the oath;
the architect who designed the Cenotaph;
which of the six was Henry the Eighth's fifth wife;
what appeared on our first Iron Age cash;
who ordered the Tower of London to be built;
where to find the National Horseracing Museum;
what, in 2007, was voted Britain's favourite view;
what, in 1944, the 'Butler Act' made law
        (though a seaside slot machine did once show me
          what it was the butler saw).

Such pub quiz ignorance is no bar against me
remaining a citizen of the UK, yet you,
who fled persecution and learned the language here,
got seven of twenty-four such questions wrong,
and so your bid to be a citizen went down.

Why should a knowledge of obscure odds and ends
of these isles' history decide your application?
Shouldn't more value be placed on understanding
and the willingness to integrate than on your capacity
to recall facts learned simply to pass a test?

You might be *au fait* with day-to-day practicalities –
what you pay for in the NHS and what you don't;
how to recycle rubbish in different-coloured bins;
how to fill in complicated forms like tax returns;
how to get on with folk from different ethnic groups –

but all these will count for naught
if, on *Life in the UK*, you score
fewer than eighteen points
out of the maximum twenty-four.

Contributors

Peter A is a Scottish writer. His poetry and short fiction have been published widely in anthologies, magazines, online and video. He won first prize in the 2016 Paisley Spree Fringe Poetry Competition. His debut chapbook, *Art of Insomnia* was published by Hedgehog Poetry Press on 31 May 2021.

Sandra A Agard has been a professional storyteller, writer, cultural historian and literary consultant for over forty years. Born in London to Guyanese parents, Sandra is the author of *Trailblazers: Harriet Tubman, A Journey to Freedom* (2019). Sandra's writing is featured in *Time for Telling* (1991), *Tales, Myths and Legends* (1991) and *Unheard Voices* (2007).

Mayo Agard-Olubo is a web designer, writer and poet based in London. In 2021, he was selected to take part in "A Writing Chance", an initiative from New Writing North. You can find more of his poetry at https://medium.com/@MayoPoetry

Advia Ahmed was born and raised in Kashmir. Now based in London and working for the NHS Mental Health Services, Advia spent nearly a year in the Calais Jungle (France) alongside Liz Clegg and other brilliant volunteers, supporting some of the most resilient human beings she has ever met.

Jim Aitken is a writer and poet who also tutors in Scottish Cultural Studies in Edinburgh. He has had his work published widely, including in the *Black Lives Matter: Poems for a New World* and he edited *A Kist of Thistles: An Anthology of Radical Poetry from Contemporary Scotland*, published by Culture Matters in 2020. He writes for the Culture Matters website and is currently editing a Scottish prose anthology for them.

Malka Al-Haddad is an Iraqi academic and poet. She has a Masters degree in Arabic Literature from Kufa University in Iraq. She is a graduate of the University of Leicester where she studied for a Master of Arts degree in the Politics of Conflict and Violence. Her debut poetry collection, *Birds Without Sky: Poems from Exile* (Harriman House Ltd, 2018) was longlisted for the Leicester Book of the Year award in 2018.

Haleemah Alaydi is a PhD researcher at the University of York. Her short story, "A Very Private Confession" was published by Valley Press in 2021 in an edited short story anthology, *This New North*. Her poems have appeared in *The Scribe*, and she has certifications in spoken word poetry.

Aryan Ashory is a 17-year-old Afghan poet, filmmaker, human rights activist and journalist. Her poems are in four languages: Dari, English, Greek and Deutsch. She volunteers with a Greek organisation as a Dari and handcrafts teacher and has made 5 shorts and documentary films. She is in charge of a women's space teaching handcrafts and English beginner classes. Aryan joined Athens Democracy Forum as a reporter in 2019 where she focuses on the voice of young people. Twitter: @AryanAshory

Janine Booth is a Marxist, trade unionist and activist, who also writes poetry! She has published several books and been included in numerous anthologies, and performs around the UK and beyond and more recently online. More here: www.janinebooth.com

Sheena Bradley was born in a small town in Derry but has now lived longer in Nottingham than elsewhere. Her work has appeared in Orbis, Indigo Dreams publications, AIOTB, Dear Reader and Impspired. Her first chapbook, *Painting My Japan* was published by Impspired in June 2021.

Lavern Buchanan-Sy (aka Nehanda) was born in Clapham, London. She is a Careers Adviser with over 30 years' experience working in this profession. She is also a mother, grandmother and daughter of parents who arrived from Jamaica to the UK in the 50s. She enjoys writing. She has contributed to a published Hair Anthology, *Hair Power - Skin Revolution*.

Helen Buckingham lives in Wells, England. Collections include *water on the moon* (original plus press, 2010) and *sanguinella* (Red Moon Press, 2017), each of which was shortlisted for a Touchstone Award. Her work appears in a number of anthologies, including *Over Land, Over Sea* (Five Leaves Publications, 2015).

Lela Burbridge is a Ugandan born Black British author living in the Cotswolds. Wife, Mother, Educator and Writer. She is also an advocate for Literacy. Website: https://www.lelaburbridge.com/

Richard Byrt has written poems on diverse topics, including past and modern slavery. He has been actively involved in poetry events in Leicester. Richard's poems are published in anthologies, Glitterwolf LGBT magazine, and in his debut collection, *Devil's Bit*, edited by Sally Jack and published by De Montfort Books.

M Chambers worked as a professional archaeologist, but is now retired. His short stories have won some prizes and have been long and shortlisted. His poetry has appeared in *Lucent Dreaming* and some anthologies. He now lives on the edge of the North York Moors.

A C Clarke's fifth collection is *A Troubling Woman*. She was a winner in the Cinnamon Press 2017 pamphlet competition with *War Baby*. *Drochaid*, with Maggie Rabatski and Sheila Templeton, was published last year. *Wedding Grief* was published as a Tapsalteerie pamphlet in June 2021.

Liz Clegg went to the Calais Jungle to drop off some aid in June 2015, she ended up staying. Alongside some awesome volunteers, Liz set up the "Unofficial" Women and Children's Centre to provide a safe space for some of the most vulnerable people in the camp.

Mark Connors is an award winning poet and novelist from Leeds, widely published in the UK and overseas. His third poetry collection, *After* was published by YAFFLE in 2021 www.markconnors.co.uk

Robin Daglish is a retired builder who discovered poetry when middle aged and has been writing poetry and short stories since. He's been published in many national and international magazines and anthologies. He self-published his first pamphlet, *Rubies*, in 2002 and his first full collection, *Weymouth Dawn* in 2012. Currently living near Brighton, he is active in the local performance poetry scene.

Catherine Davidson is a dual UK/US citizen, member of the board of Exiled Writers Ink, an organisation supporting exiled and refugee writers, a pro-immigration campaigner, and a published poet. She has put out two pamphlets with UK presses, has published in both countries and most recently, has had poems selected in an anthology edited by Ann Sampson, and another by Eleni Cay. Occasional prizes include, most recently, a Troubadour International long list, and a Free Verse prize.

Emer Davis, born in Ireland, has lived in London, Abu Dhabi and New Delhi. She has worked on the EU Relocation Programme on Lesvos Island in 2016. She was runner up in the 2018 Trocaire Poetry Ireland Poetry competition for her poem Raqqa Bowl 2017. She has three collections published: *Kill Your Television, Chaat* and *Postcards from India*. Further information on her poems can be found on Bunnacurrypoet.org.

John Davison is a London-born writer of parodies, poems and lyrics, often on topical issues. He admires unusual puns and wordplay and frequents open mics in outer London, collaborating with musicians whenever opportunities present themselves. He supports a Twitter account https://twitter.com/sidsaucer and the geo-locational poetry site https://www.placesofpoetry.org.uk/

Theoni Dourida is a drama teacher who lives in Athens, Greece. She likes observing the world around her and sometimes writes poems and short stories about it. Hopefully, in the near future, she will follow her love and dreams in the UK.

Alan Dunnett's collection, *A Third Colour* was published by Culture Matters in 2018. He wrote/voiced the film-poem *Interrogation*, Best Experimental Film at the Verona International Film Festival 2019. "Shot in the Head", informed by *Narratives from Columbians Displaced by Violence*, is in *The Very Edge* (Flying Ketchup Press, 2020). The poem-film *Clytemnestra* was selected for The Film & Video Poetry Symposium 2021.

Attracta Fahy, Psychotherapist, MAW NUIG '17. Winner of Trócaire Poetry Ireland Poetry Competition 2021. Irish Times; New Irish Writing 2019, Pushcart & Best of Web nominee, shortlisted for: OTE 2018 New Writer, Allingham Poetry competition both 2019 &'20, and Write By The Sea Writing Competition 2021. Her poems have been published in many magazines at home and abroad. Attracta was chosen for Dedalus Press Mentoring Programme 2021. Fly on the Wall Poetry published her bestselling debut chapbook collection, *Dinner in the Fields*, in March '20.

Max Terry Fishel. Born Liverpool, resides London. Jew-ish. Plays Irish music, writes poems, worries about hair loss. Mainly analogue, partly digital. Enjoys performing at open mics. "You can lead a horse to water, but you can't pull the wool up the garden path" – how true this is. Thinks love is best.

Paul Francis is a retired teacher, living in Much Wenlock. He is a versatile and prolific poet, active in the West Midlands poetry scene, who has won national prizes. In spring 2021, he had two collections published – *Rescue from the Dark* (Fair Acre Press) and *Dreams of Brexit* (Liberty Books).

Birgit Friedrich is a German national writing poetry and fiction in English. She recently achieved a Distinction in her MA studies in creative writing at Nottingham Trent University and writes passionately about the everyday lives of mature women. She is currently working on her first novel.

Stephanie Goodacre has worked in the voluntary sector in Leicester for over three decades supporting vulnerable young people and families. She discovered a love of writing poetry about 10 years ago at The Percival Guildhouse, Rugby. Her interests range from local traditions to the global environment and are reflected in two pamphlets: *Household Geology* and *Liquid Geography*.

Anne Goodwin's fiction focuses on identity, mental health and social justice. Her debut novel, *Sugar and Snails*, was shortlisted for the 2016 Polari First Book Prize. Her new novel, *Matilda Windsor Is Coming Home* is inspired by her work in a long-stay psychiatric hospital. Website: annegoodwin.weebly.com

Barrington Gordon, is a published author. He's published in *Voice Memory Ashes: Lest We Forget*, a short story called "The Chair". His short story, "Grandfather's Feet" was published in *Whispers in the Walls*, a Birmingham anthology, endorsed by Bonnie Greer and Benjamin Zephaniah. BBC Radio 4 also featured this tale.

GPT-2 is a deep learning model from OpenAI that was fine-tuned on a 1.2MB text file containing poems from Maya Angelou, Robert Frost, Jane Campion, Roald Dahl and William Blake.
https://openai.com/blog/tags/gpt-2/

Joachim Grevel is a scientist, whose life as a foreigner started at the age of 12: Germany, Austria, United States, Switzerland, Scotland, Italy, England. He took the pledge to the Queen in Leicester, but Brexit turned the table on him, and he is a foreigner again.

Laura Grevel is a performance poet, fiction writer and blogger. Originally from Texas, she has lived in Europe for 20 years. Her work is eclectic, encompassing the immigrant experience, narratives, nature and character sketches. Her latest collaborative YouTube video is *Girl Walking Across Europe by Poets For Refugees*. Google Laura Grevel YouTube for her performances. Website: www.lgrevel.org Blog: https://lgrevel.wordpress.com

Originally from the Philippines, **Rosario Guimba-Stewart** came to England in 1995. Her first job in the UK was for the Refugee Council and in 2010, she joined the Lewisham Refugee and Migrant Network (LRMN) as their CEO. The experience of the people who came to LRMN was her inspiration in writing her poems.

Monique Guz became a UK citizen in 2020 (it took 7 visas), making her a Filipina-American Brit. She is currently writing a book about her US-UK experiences as an immigrant descended from immigrants and was recently mentored by the National Centre for Writing's Escalator scheme. She is also a pianist.

Kim Hackleman is a lover of peace, mother of boys, writer, director, actor and producer.

Born in Hungary, **Zsófia Hacsek** migrated to Austria in 2010 and then to the UK in 2018. She works at Coventry University. Her passion for her native language made her maintain strong ties with the Hungarian literary scene, being the author of several creative and journalistic publications herself.

Nusrat Haider works in children's residential services in a local authority. She has contributed to the following anthologies: *Leicester 2084 AD: New Poems about The City*; *Bollocks to Brexit: an Anthology of Poems and Short Fiction*; *Black Lives Matter: Poems for a New World* and *Wondering Souls*. In her free time, Nusrat loves to spend time with family, cooking, crafts, reading and walking, seeking rural landscapes.

Steve Harrison from Yorkshire now lives in Shropshire. His work has been published in The Emergency Poet collections, The Physic Garden, Pop Shot, Wetherspoons News, HCE, Strix, several on-line sites and appears on YouTube as steveharrisonpoet. He performs across the Midlands and The Marches and won the Ledbury Poetry Festival Slam in 2014.

Etzali Hernández is a nonbinary latinx queer fierce femme poet, coder, DJ, No Borders organiser, and social justice trainer. Their work has been published in Ascend Magazine, *We Were Always Here: A Queer Words Anthology*, and *Ceremony* (Scottish BAME Writers Network). Etzali's first poetry pamphlet is forthcoming from Forest Publications. Website: www.panditita.uk

Alice Herve coordinates the language support for the volunteer-led charity, Bath Welcomes Refugees. She writes poetry, fiction and non-fiction and has a PhD in Literature and Creative Writing.

Angi Holden is a retired lecturer, whose published work includes adult and children's poetry, short stories and flash fictions. Her pamphlet,

Spools of Thread won the Mother's Milk Pamphlet Prize. In 2019, she won the Victoria Baths Splash Fiction competition and was placed in the Cheshire Prize for Literature competition.

Leila M.J is an Iranian woman who enjoys writing short stories and poetry. She was encouraged to start writing by her English teacher, Catherine Hartley, from SWVG (Southampton and Winchester Visitors Group).

Kevin Qweaver Jackson, based in East Midlands, UK, has been writing and performing for over 10 years. A queer community and social rights activist, he revels in poetry's subversion, its ways of opening minds. He has three published collections, *Slantwise*, the most recent, came out from Bearded Badger Publishing in September 2021, to wide acclaim (Beardedbadgerpublishing.com). He performs widely and is a proud member of Nottingham's DIY Poets collective. Kevin blogs at https://www.facebook.com/kevinjacksonpoetry

Cynthia Rodríguez Juárez is a multidisciplinary writer and performer. Born in Monterrey, México but based in Leicester, she has a double citizenship but does not believe in borders. Her debut poetry collection, *Meanwhile*, was released in 2020 by Burning Eye Books. http://www.cynthiarodriguez.org

athina k is in a permanent midlife crisis and writes poetry to battle the horror of everyday life in England.

Orphée Kashala is a Creative Producer, curator and writer, originally from the Democratic Republic of Congo, currently based in Leicester. His recent creative work is centered around highlighting the thoughts, feelings and emotions of refugees and migrants in the UK. He curated an exhibition in September 2021 titled "Survivor's Guilt" as part of Coventry City of Culture 2021.

Margaret Kiernan of Mullingar, County Westmeath, Ireland, writes poetry and short stories. She has a professional background in Advocacy and Social Justice. She is published, for poetry and creative fiction. She is currently a Nominee for The Best of The Net, 2021. She writes with Over the Edge, at Galway City. She has four grown-up sons and lives with her dog, Mollie. She is a landscape painter.

Rob Lowe continues to write and publish mainly political poems in the hope that doing so changes himself, his readers, and perhaps even aspects of the world. Emily Dickinson, Nazim Hikmet and Edith Sodergran remain major influences on his work. Latterly, he has begun studying Derek Walcott.

Monica Manolachi is a writer, literary translator and lecturer at the University of Bucharest, Romania. She is the author of *Performative Identities in Contemporary Caribbean British Poetry* (2017) and has published many academic articles on contemporary literature in English. Her latest work, *Brasília* (2019), is co-authored with Neil Leadbeater.

Carmina Masoliver is a London poet, founder of She Grrrowls and has been sharing her poetry on both the page and stage for over a decade, and her latest book, *Circles* is published by Burning Eye Books (2019). @CarminaPoetry   www.carminamasoliver.com   @shegrrrowls www.shegrrrowls.com

Gia Mawusi was born in Mozambique and works in Community Projects in Great Yarmouth. She writes poetry and fiction. "My Land" featured in *Field Work: New Nature Writing from East Anglia,* and her poems in *No Relevance*, Red Herring Press. She participated in the High Street Tales Project.

Jenny Mitchell is winner of the International Poetry Book Awards 2021 for her second collection, *Map of a Plantation*. It was chosen as a

"Literary Find" in the Irish Independent and a Poetry Kit Book of the Month. She has won the Ware, Folklore and Aryamati Prizes, and a Bread and Roses Award as well as several other competitions. A debut collection, *Her Lost Language*, was voted "One of 44 Books of 2019" (Poetry Wales). She has just been made Artist in Association at Birkbeck, University of London.

Mehrzad Mohamadi was born in Shiraz, Iran, which is known as the capital of Persian literature and poetry. Due to his interest in the poems of Rumi, Saadi and Ferdowsi, he chose the field of Persian literature, from which he graduated at the age of 18. Mehrzad is proud to be part of Good Chance's Change the Word poetry collective in the UK.

Hubert Moore's eleventh full collection appeared in April 2021. It's called *Owl Songs*. His last six collections have all contained poems which express his concern for refugees in the UK. Between 2000 and 2010, he was a writing mentor with Freedom from Torture and a visitor at Dover Immigration Detention Centre.

Yasin Moradi is originally Kurdish from Iran and came to live in England in 2015. He now lives in London as an actor, stand-up comedian and martial arts teacher. He performed with Good Chance Theatre in the multi-award winning, internationally-acclaimed play, *The Jungle*. He is a member of Good Chance's Change the Word Poetry Collective.

Cheryl Moskowitz is a writer, educator and creative translator with a background in theatre and psychoanalysis. She runs projects in the community, including in prisons, with the homeless and with refugees. Book publications include novel, *Wyoming Trail* (Granta); poetry collection, *The Girl is Smiling* (Circle Time Press); poetry for children, *Can it Be About Me?* (Frances Lincoln Books) and poetry pamphlet, *Maternal Impression* (Against the Grain).

Loraine Mponela is a Malawian mother, writer, former lecturer, community organiser and migrants' rights campaigner. She moved to England in 2008. Her poems and articles have been published in several books, anthologies, online magazines, blogs and videos around the world including The Guardian Foundation, Liquid Amber Press, Cambridge University Press, *the other side of hope*, and more. Loraine has a lovely son, Comfort. Loraine's "No Audience" Youtube channel is available at https://www.youtube.com/channel/UC9rXX-OPIAZh2y67uFDQN8A

Ambrose Musiyiwa is a poet and a journalist. He coordinates Journeys in Translation, an international, volunteer-driven initiative that is translating *Over Land, Over Sea: Poems for those seeking* refuge (Five Leaves Publications, 2015) into other languages. Books he has edited include *Bollocks to Brexit: an Anthology of Poems and Short Fiction* (2019) and *Black Lives Matter: Poems for a New World* (2020).

Chad Norman lives and writes in Truro, Nova Scotia. His poems appear in publications around the world. His latest book, *Simona: A Celebration of the S.P.C.A.* is published by Cyberwit.net, out of India.

Sarah Nymanhall lives and writes in Bristol, UK. She is a third generation descendant of Polish, Russian and Welsh immigrants. As someone who values the expressive power of the spoken word, she mourns the mother tongue languages of Yiddish and Welsh lost to her during her families' migratory journeys.

Denise O'Hagan is an award-winning editor and poet. She has a background in commercial book publishing. In 2015, she set up her own imprint, Black Quill Press, through which she assists independent authors. Her poetry is published widely and has received numerous awards, most recently the Dalkey Poetry Prize 2020. https://denise-ohagan.com

Catherine Okoronkwo, of Nigerian heritage, grew up in the Middle East and studied in the USA and UK. She holds an MA with distinction and PhD in Creative Writing. Her work has been anthologised in *Elevator Fiction* (2016), *Crossings Over* (2017), *Black Lives Matter: Poems for a New World* (2020) and *Where We Find Ourselves* (2021). Her debut collection, *Blood and Water ọbara na mmiri* is published by Waterloo Press (2020). She serves as a Church of England priest in the South-West.

David Owen is an academic at the University of Southampton who works in migration and refugee studies. His most recent book is *What Do We Owe to Refugees?* (Polity 2020). He is also a very minor published poet.

S. Muge Ozbay (Born in Istanbul, lives in London). Walks, swims, dances, draws and writes. Studied literature, art and visual cultures in Istanbul and London. Worked as a tour guide in the past.

Nasrin Parvaz became a civil rights activist when the Islamic regime took power in 1979. She was arrested in 1982, and spent eight years in prison. Her books are, *One Woman's Struggle in Iran, a Prison Memoir*, and *The Secret Letters from X to A* (Victorina Press, 2018). http://nasrinparvaz.org/

Pascale Petit was born in Paris and lives in Cornwall. She is of French, Welsh, and Indian heritage. Her eighth collection, *Tiger Girl* (Bloodaxe Books, 2020), was shortlisted for the Forward Prize and for Wales Book of the Year. Her seventh collection, *Mama Amazonica* (Bloodaxe Books, 2017), won the inaugural Laurel Prize for eco-poetry, the Royal Society of Literature's Ondaatje Prize, and was a Poetry Book Society Choice. Four previous collections were shortlisted for the T.S. Eliot Prize.

Stephanie Powell grew up in Melbourne, Australia. She has spent the last few years living in London (with some short stints in Canada and Kenya).

She writes and takes photos. Her collection *Bone* was published by Halas Press in July 2021.

Jova Bagioli Reyes is an unapologetically queer, latinx, and political poet and musician. An immigrant from day one and coming from countries that have suffered dictatorships and colonization, they explore topics such as anti-colonialism, struggle, and liberation with their work, seeking to foster solidarity amongst all peoples. They are part of the Manchester poetry collective Young Identity and are known for challenging the status quo. You can find more of their poetry and music under their pseudonym, *Jova and the Wave*.

Kay Ritchie grew up in Glasgow and Edinburgh, lived in London, Spain and Portugal and worked as a freelance photographer and radio producer. Published in magazines and anthologies in the UK, Ireland and Africa, she has performed at events like Aye Write, Women's Aid Billion Women Rising and the Edinburgh Fringe.

Richard Roe lives in Nuneaton, England. Having worked for a number of charities, mainly associated with asylum seekers and the homeless, he is now a freelance citizen helping people in the community. Several poems have been published in anthologies. *Prisoners of Beliefs* is his first book out in December 2021. The characters are fictional but the events are factual. The book exposes how all our beliefs distort reality poisoning the next generation. The hero is a Black African.

Caroline Rooney was born in Zimbabwe and currently lives in London. She is an arts activist and filmmaker, and she is a researcher in the field of liberation movements. Her latest book is *Creative Radicalism in the Middle East: Culture and the Arab Left After the Uprisings* (I.B. Tauris, 2020).

K J Rowswell writes poetry and fiction. His work reflects two major themes: the human condition and humankind's relationship with the environment. He has performed and broadcast his work. Based in Scotland, he is also an advocate of Scottish Gaelic and the Scots language in writing and performance.

Burak Şahin has been living in the UK for nine years and is originally from Turkey. He works in an immigration law company, and his family also moved to Switzerland around five years ago. He has first-hand experience about the immigration processes through himself, his family and through his work.

Barbara Saunders' work appears in anthologies such as *Black Lives Matter: Poems for a New World* (CivicLeicester), *Can You Hear the People Sing?* (Palewell Press) and *Over Land, Over Sea: Poems for those seeking refuge* (Five Leaves). It also appears in The Journal and Exiled Ink online. Her grandparents were Jewish Russians who immigrated before The Aliens Act of 1905.

Maggie Sawkins is the recipient of the 2013 Ted Hughes Award for New Work in Poetry for *Zones of Avoidance*, a sequence of poems inspired by her personal and professional involvement with people in recovery from addictions. Maggie's most recent project was "Community Conversations", a series of poetry workshops and performances with the refugee and asylum seeker community in Portsmouth. www.hookedonwords.wordpress.com

Ian Seed's collections of poetry and prose poetry include *The Underground Cabaret* (Shearsman, 2020), *Operations of Water* (Knives, Forks and Spoons Press, 2020) and *New York Hotel* (Shearsman, 2018) (*Times Literary Supplement* Book of the Year 2018). His most recent translation is *Bitter Grass* (Shearsman, 2020), from the Italian of Gëzim Hajdari.

Suzan Criscentia Spence is a playwright, actor and poet based in the UK, West Midlands. As the artistic director of the theatre company, Drama and Some CIC, she has had several plays produced, with some emphasis on social comment. An active member of several writers' groups, including, West Bromwich Writers Group; Writers Without Borders and Poets' Place, her poetry has been published in books and pamphlets, as well as online. It gave her particular satisfaction to be selected for publication in the *Black Lives Matter: Poems for a New World* anthology from CivicLeicester, as she previously lived and worked in Leicester as a Registered General Nurse. https://www.dramaandsome.org/

Paul Stephenson has published three pamphlets: *Those People* (Smith/Doorstop), *The Days that Followed Paris* (HappenStance) and *Selfie with Waterlilies* (Paper Swans Press). He co-edited Magma issue 70 on "Europe". He co-curates Poetry in Aldeburgh and currently lives between Cambridge and Brussels, where he walks the city taking photos of incredible doors. Instagram: paulstep456. Twitter: @stephenson_pj / www.paulstep.com

Diliana Stoyanova is a Bulgarian-Finnish spoken-word and sound poet, and PhD candidate based in Helsinki. A 2019 Finnish national slam finalist and an avid online slammer, she writes to take ownership of her own narrative.

Marie-Therese Taylor's works can be read in *The Glasgow Review of Books, Ink Sweat and Tears, The Interpreter's House, Northwords Now, The Lake, Under the Radar*, and *Poems for Grenfell*. She won first prize in *Mountaineering Scotland 2019* poetry competition, and in Nottingham University's project concerning male eating disorders. She lives in Glasgow, a city which is much concerned with the issue of asylum.

Angela Topping is the author of eight full poetry collections and four pamphlets. Her work has appeared in a wide range of journals and anthologies. She is a former Writer in Residence at Gladstone's Library.

Lauren Tormey is an American-born immigrant who moved to Scotland in 2011. Since being granted Indefinite Leave to Remain in 2020, she has been campaigning for a more humane immigration system in the UK. Her poem, "Temporary" describes her lived experience at the start of the coronavirus pandemic.

Lytisha Tunbridge is a Nottingham based writer, runs creative writing workshops with Poetry Aloud, and is a member of both World Jam and DIY Poets collectives. More can be found at https://lytishapoet.co.uk

Deborah Tyler-Bennett is a European writer who has work published in a variety of new anthologies and journals, as well as having had eight volumes of poetry and three of linked short stories published. In 2021, she won the adult section of Writing East Midlands'/ Derbyshire Wildlife Trust's "Ghosts of the Landscape" Competition with her poem, "The Ash Woman Speaks". New work has dealt with themes of ecology, folklore, and those perceived as being on society's margins.

PR Walker lives in North London. He started writing poetry again in 2018 after a gap of over 30 years. Over the past two years, he's had several poems shortlisted/commended in competitions or published in magazines and anthologies, including *The New European*, *Honest Ulsterman* and *Black Lives Matter: Poems for a New World*. His recent poem, "The Grammar of the World is losing its Syntax" was runner up in the 2021 Desmond O'Grady International Poetry Competition.

Gail Webb is originally from Wales, now living in Nottingham. She is a member of DIY Poets, Poetry Crane Collective, World Jam and GOBS Collective. She writes to share experiences, to make sense of a hurting world and find some joy in the small things. Published in Boshemia Journal 2019, and several anthologies.

Patricia Welles has published 6 novels; had readings of her plays - one produced at Hampstead Theatre (London); published poetry, book reviews; achieved a Master's Degree in Psychoanalysis; sold her first novel to Columbia Pictures (Sony); wrote the novelization of a comedy film, *Bob&Carol&Ted&Alice* and just completed her first screenplay. Her advice is to "keep going".

Richard Williams lives in Portsmouth. Poetry in a wide range of magazines, first collection, *Landings*, published by Dempsey & Windle in 2018. Organised Poetry of Exile film poem screenings on the BBC Big Screens in Portsmouth and Dover and writing workshops in Haslar Immigration Removal Centre. Blogs at www.richardwilliamspoetry.com

Kimmika Williams-Witherspoon, PhD (Cultural Anthropology), M.A. (Anthropology), MFA (Theater), Graduate Certificate (Women's Studies), B.A. (Journalism); is an Associate Professor of Urban Theater and Community Engagement at Temple. Author of *Through Smiles and Tears* (2011) and *The Secret Messages in African American Theater* (2006), she has had over 29 plays produced.

Michele Witthaus has settled in Leicester, UK, having called several countries home, including South Africa, Canada and Cyprus. Her pamphlet, *From a Sheltered Place* was published in August 2020 by Wild Pressed Books. She has poems in several anthologies and other publications and is the 2020 winner of Leicester Writers' Club's Ena Young Award for Poetry and Chris D'Lacey Endeavour Award.

Gregory Woods is the author of six poetry collections from Carcanet Press, the latest being *Records of an Incitement to Silence* (2021). His main books of gay cultural history are published by Yale University Press.

He is Emeritus Professor of Gay and Lesbian Studies at Nottingham Trent University.

Mantz Yorke lives in Manchester, England. His poems have been published both in the UK and internationally. His collections, *Voyager* and *Dark Matters* are published by Dempsey & Windle.

Acknowledgements

Acknowledgements and thanks to all who distributed our call for submissions, and to all who responded, and to Richard Byrt for proofreading the final manuscript.

Some of the poems in this anthology have been published previously as follows –

"The Citizens of Nowhere" by Jim Aitken, in the magazine, *Southlight*, Issue 28, 2020

"The Trip of Death & Shattered Hopes" by Saffanna Al Jbawi, in Hernandez, E. (2021). The Politics of Being a Writer: In Conversation with Saffana Al Jbawi. In Scottish BAME Writers Network (2022) www.scottishbamewritersnetwork.org/the-politics-of-being-a-writer/

"Another Country" by Janine Booth in Janine Booth (2016), at janinebooth.com, 5 December 2016 www.janinebooth.com/content/another-country

"Haiku" by Helen Buckingham, in *brass bell: a haiku journal* (ed. Z. Zahava, 1 March, 2017) www.brassbellhaiku.blogspot.com/2017/03

"What a performance" by A C Clarke, in *War Baby* (Cinnamon Press, 2018)

"Letter to Jamil" by Liz Clegg. Read on YouTube by Liz Clegg (Choose Love, 22 February 2016) https://youtu.be/T2qZ6gfu_BY

"All Aboard" by Mark Connors, in *Nothing is Meant to be Broken* (Stairwell Books, 2017)

"Succour" by Alan Dunnett, in *The Best New British and Irish Poets 2016* (Eyewear, 2016)

"Beautiful One" by Attracta Fahy, in *Abridged Literary Magazine Northern Ireland*, in 2020

"My Mother Smoking" by Max Terry Fishel. Read on YouTube by Max Terry Fishel (Peter Murry, 14 September 2021) https://youtu.be/UPgJk0FBjF0

"Girl Walking Across Europe" by Laura Grevel. Written by Laura Grevel and read on YouTube by several poets (Laura Grevel, 17 March 2021) https://youtu.be/Worbl_atBtU

"Rite of Passage" by Zsófia Hacsek, in Hungarian as "Átmeneti rítus", on the blog of the Hungarian literature group, Yriunk, on 12 September 2019 https://yriunk.blogspot.com/2019/09/hacsek-zsofia-atmeneti-ritus.html

"Transit Centre" by Angi Holden, in *Writers for Calais Refugees* (ed. Marie Lightman) https://writersforcalaisrefugees.wordpress.com

"Her Lost Language" by Jenny Mitchell, in *Her Lost Language* by (Indigo Dreams, 2019)

"Tonight" by Mehrzad Mohamadi, in *Change the Word: Poems from Barnsley and Beyond* (Good Chance, 2021)

"I come from" by Yasin Moradi, in *Change the Word: Poems from Barnsley and Beyond* (Good Chance, 2021)

"Asylum" by Cheryl Moskowitz, *The Girl is Smiling* (Circle Time Press, 2012)

"Do not give me Indefinite Leave to Remain when I lose my mental capacity" by Loraine Masiya Mponela. Read on YouTube by Loraine Masiya Mponela (Loraine Mponela, 14 June 2021) https://youtu.be/hh66LnJZBQg

"Do not let Bukhary be forgotten" by Loraine Masiya Mponela. Read on YouTube by Loraine Masiya Mponela (Loraine Mponela, 19 July 2021) https://youtu.be/MjuLeIpq9AQ

"Penny Walker" by Loraine Masiya Mponela. Read on YouTube by Loraine Masiya Mponela (Loraine Mponela, 21 June 2021) https://youtu.be/BKhkh3hR3Hk

"Martians. Effing Martians" by Ambrose Musiyiwa, in Sam Smith's *The Journal* (once '*of Contemporary Anglo-Scandinavian Poetry*'), Issue 49

"The Quiet Assimilators" by Denise O'Hagan, a longer version, in *Eureka Street*, Vol. 29, No. 18, 8 September 2019 http://www.eurekastreet.com.au/article/the-quiet-assimilators

"Passport" by Pascale Petit, in *Tiger Girl* by Pascale Petit (Bloodaxe 2020)

"Mr Nobody" by Burak Sahin in *the other side of hope: journeys in refugee and immigrant literature* (eds. Alexandros Plasatis *et al*, 2021). www.othersideofhope.com/burak-sahin-mr-nobody.html

"Teaching English at Friendship House" by Maggie Sawkins in *The Zig Zag Woman* by Maggie Sawkins (Two Ravens Press, 2007).

"Rome" by Ian Seed, in *The Underground Cabaret* by Ian Seed (Shearsman Books, 2020)

"The Danish Vote" by Paul Stephenson, in *The Fenland Reed*

"Citizenship Test" by Marie-Therese Taylor, in *To Whom It May Concern: Letters of Petition to Mark the 700th Anniversary of the Declaration of Arbroath* (Federation of Writers Scotland, 2021)

"This Land" by Ursula Troche, with a video, in *North East Bylines* (1 July 2021) https://northeastbylines.co.uk/this-land/

"Ask Yourself" by Lytisha Tunbridge, in *Visual Verse: an Anthology of Art and Words* (eds. Preti Taneji and Lucie Stevens. Vol 8, Chapter 05, (March 2021) https://visualverse.org/submissions/ask-yourself/

"Your Side of the Pond" by Deborah Tyler-Bennett, in *London Grip* (Autumn 2019)

"The Transmutation of Geese" by Richard Williams, in *Landings* by Richard Williams (Dempsey & Windle, 2018)

"No Trivial Pursuit" by Mantz Yorke, in *Quaranzine* (13 June 2021) www.thirdestate.org/quaranzine/no-trivial-pursuit-by-mantz-yorke

Financial Support

Acknowledgements and thanks to all who pledged financial support for this project and enabled us to meet some of the costs associated with bringing the anthology out. https://gofund.me/fd9c2b6b

The support is much appreciated.

Printed in Great Britain
by Amazon